Praise

'Harnessing the passion and expertise of your employees can be a game-changer, and this book brilliantly illustrates how to do just that. Whether you're a seasoned marketer looking to amplify your brand's reach or a people and culture leader striving to cultivate a culture of employee engagement and advocacy, this book is a great resource.'
   — **Kamila Hutchison**, Group Go-To-Market Lead, CHG-MERIDIAN, Australia

'An indispensable resource for enterprise social marketing teams, marketing leaders and anyone interested in making LinkedIn work for their business, this book offers a thorough exploration of the strategies and practical actions required to unlock employee brand influencers. Readers will discover an impeccably crafted blueprint, a pragmatic roadmap, and a time-efficient 10-hour action plan for the launch of a robust LinkedIn program. Dive into this essential guide and unlock the full potential of your LinkedIn endeavours.'
   — **Ross Gearing**, Head of Marketing, Maersk, Asia Pacific

'This guide has been an invaluable asset to me. It underscores the importance of employee influencers at all levels, the emphasis on native and organic approaches, and the essence of brand advocacy.'
   — **Oliver Leon**, Digital Strategist, Pen & Paper, Central Europe

'I wish this book was available when I joined LinkedIn. It's the perfect guide to making the best out of your and your colleagues' LinkedIn performance.'
— **Ján Haraslín**, Community Manager, European Parliament Liaison Office in SVK

'This book is an absolute game-changer. It lays out a slick 10-hour Ambassador Launch Plan, turning your colleagues into LinkedIn rockstars for your brand. The authors shine a spotlight on the untapped goldmine within your team and reveal the steep cost of missing out. This book is your backstage pass to boosting talent and creating transformative partnerships.'
— **Juraj Polerecký**, Enterprise Segment Marketing Lead at Microsoft Central and Eastern Europe, Middle East and Africa

THE MAGIC OF

Activate your Employee Ambassadors
on LinkedIn™ to enhance branding,
boost sales and attract top talent

EMPLOYEE INFLUENCE

IVANA BRUTENIČ, PhD
KRISTÍNA CICHÝ KOVÁČIKOVÁ, PhD

R^ethink

First published in Great Britain in 2024
by Rethink Press (www.rethinkpress.com)

© Copyright Ivana Brutenič, Kristína Cichý Kováčiková

For our heroes

Disclaimer

This book represents our experience and should not be interpreted as legal, economic, business, financial, health, or any form of professional advice.

You either see a great potential in Employee Ambassadors, or you have been given a task to choose them. An Ambassador Project needs to be individually tailored to your company needs. Results will vary depending on your starting point, type of business, level of experience and time and energy level you are willing to put into this project. None of the author(s), publisher(s), distributor(s) or copyright holder(s) provides any form of representations or warranties with respect to the contents of the book and/or use of the networks, services and/or other products and/or activities, attitudes, methods or ideas described in this book. Representations and warranties are provided neither with respect to any accuracy or completeness of the contents of this book nor with respect to its suitability for your specific situations or needs. No warranty is provided and no warranty can be extended by any third party. None of the author(s), publisher(s), distributor(s) or copyright holder(s) shall be liable for any loss or damages, including but not limited to any loss of profit, direct or indirect, consequential, special or incidental damages.

LinkedIn is the registered trademark of LinkedIn Corporation or its affiliates. The use of the LinkedIn trademark in connection with this product does not signify any affiliation with or endorsement by LinkedIn Corporation or its affiliates.

Contents

Introduction   1

1 Get Your Colleagues On Board   9

What is buy-in and why do you need it?   10
What is the Ambassador Project?   13
Social media platforms and Employee
Ambassadors   16
Are you ready?   20
Risks of having Ambassadors   22
Safeguarding your company's reputation   24
Setting the Project goals and measuring results   27
Summary   32

2 Ambassador Volunteers   33

The four roles of the Ambassador Project   34

Managing expectations   44

The unique Ambassador's adventure   45

Promoting the Ambassador role   47

How to select Ambassadors   48

Content guidelines for Ambassadors   51

How to manage those not selected   55

Summary   56

3 Content Creation Is Full Of Opportunities   59

What is content creation?   60

Top ten content challenges and solutions   61

Nervous system response and its impact on
content creation   73

Evergreen content   78

Summary   81

4 Practical Content Creation   83

Define the Lead   83

Create content that converts   86

LinkedIn algorithm   88

The 5-ingredient method for content creation   91

Content hubs – the secret to staying
organised   97

Artificial Intelligence for content creation   103

Summary   106

5 Unique Structure For Your LinkedIn Presence   107

Structures for the best results   108

Personal profile vs Company Page
(reaching vs anchoring)   114

Potential risks and how to avoid them   118

Global Ambassadors and your LinkedIn
presence   123

Summary   125

6 The 10-hour Launch Plan   **127**

A (love) letter to the Project Hero   127

The detailed plan   128

Summary   146

7 Think Big, Think Global   **147**

The tone of voice and cultural differences   148

Start planning   149

Common questions   151

Global Ambassador Project roles   155

5-step process for the Global Superhero   160

10-hour Launch Plan modified for a global
impact   162

Make a difference with a global impact   166

Summary   170

Conclusion   **171**

Resources   **175**

Acknowledgements   **177**

The Authors   **179**

Introduction

The secret weapon that can dramatically pivot your company's trajectory lies closer than you think. Tap into the power hiding in plain sight and transform your own colleagues into powerful brand voices.

You are reading this book because you already know there is an untapped potential of Employee Ambassadors in your company. Maybe you have seen your competitors' content performing well and feel the urge to act. You know that Employee Ambassadors can attract clients and talent and maybe you want that at the snap of your fingers, but you don't know how to make that magic happen.

When you work with people who love their jobs, you have an army of colleagues who can tap into opportunities you are missing. But do you know the cost of not using your employees' network to attract talent and business partnerships? For some, that could be thousands of pounds or dollars; for others, millions of euros and more.

Imagine that you have a simple way that could help your colleagues significantly increase:

- Their morale and motivation

- Their appreciation of your company culture and benefits

- Their sense of pride and ownership in your company's success

- How your company culture shows up in their day-to-day life

- How the market perceives your company through your values

- The number of clients and new talent that come your way

- The trust that your customers and clients have in your brand

- The ability to influence and manage your own and your company's reputation

Your colleagues spend hours every day browsing social media. What if you could focus their time and help them become creators instead of consumers, bringing your company opportunities you need, and some you may not have even thought of? They need a straightforward system that turns mindless browsing into a powerful and well-defined Employee Ambassador adventure. Otherwise, they are wasting their own and the company's time.

When you get a task to start an Ambassador Project and your own career success is tied into it, forget just encouraging people to post on LinkedIn randomly. Without giving them the right tools and a formal process to follow, they become more open to talent hunters. Then they get headhunted! They leave the company having wasted time and failed to help the business progress and generate income.

There is a better way. We are sisters Kristína and Ivana, raised in the heart of Europe, Slovakia. We joined forces in 2015 and created the first consultancy for building brands on LinkedIn in Slovakia, rebranding it to SUNDAYFLIES in 2022. For over a decade, we have empowered our clients to use their voices to attract opportunities and talent systematically and in record time, while still having fun. In this book, we share our 10-hour Ambasador Launch Plan that will make it easier to empower your colleagues and focus their social media activity so that your company can achieve its goals.

We created this Plan because we have seen countless companies struggle to set up a formal Ambassador Project for months, even years. We know how to turn your colleagues' random acts of social into a stream-lined, fun and proven process and we would love you to take it and use it to reach your goals. You can have many goals, and we will help you define them along the way. For example, you may want to show the world:

- That you are the most innovative in your industry

- That your company is a great place to work for the top talent in your niche

- The exact solutions you have for your potential clients

The 10-hour Launch Plan for LinkedIn is a proven system which creates strong brands that people love, want to partner, do business with and get a job at. We passionately take our clients through LinkedIn journeys that:

- Create ten times the LinkedIn following of corporations

- Scale small- and medium-sized companies through large projects generated from LinkedIn

- Attract journalists and podcasters so that our clients are featured on TV, in newspapers and magazines as an additional bonus to getting new projects, talent and clients

In this book, we will show you how to tap into the limitless power of your colleagues' voices. The tool we use is LinkedIn because, it is the most trusted social media platform and full of business opportunities. For five years LinkedIn has ranked as the most trusted social media in the US, according to eMarketer's Digital Trust Benchmark Report 2021.[1] We have seen so much magic happen through this platform. We will take you on an adventure, and at the end, you will have a plan for launching your Ambassador Project in just 10 hours. You can achieve a month's worth of work by the end of this week.

The patterns we saw for over a decade have led us to create and implement our signature Employee Ambassadors Framework. It works across various business models: B2B, B2C, B2G, large corporations and small businesses, worldwide. In this book, you will learn how to make the launch of your own Ambassador Project as quick and enjoyable as possible.

You do not have to spend months or years thinking about Employee Ambassadors and trying to guess what will work. You do not need to create the strategy yourself or learn more about LinkedIn. We've done all the hard work for you, so you can focus on what's essential: reaching your goals.

---

1   A Schomer, D Aho Williamson, *Digital Trust Benchmark Report 2021* (25 October 2021), www.insiderintelligence.com/content/digital-trust-benchmark-report-2021, accessed 19 September 2023

In an increasingly automated world, the human being becomes the factor that makes the difference. You must select the right colleagues for the right roles during this Project, and we will teach you how. That is the heavy lifting to get this Project going for years.

That is why we love to work on these projects with our clients. We have witnessed how people's lives have changed because of using their voices as Employee Ambassadors. For example:

- Million-dollar projects generated through Employee Ambassadors' content
- 300,000 euros a year generated in free media coverage and business partnerships
- CEOs, HR and marketing professionals and other specialists becoming more influential by winning awards
- Non-profits winning support from affluent donors
- Various departments and locations miraculously start communicating and solving each other's problems
- Getting recognition and awards like The Employer of the Year, The HR Talent of the Year or The Best LinkedIn Profile in a particular niche

- Small businesses securing large clients they dreamed of in just 30 days of an active Ambassador Project

It doesn't matter if you are in a huge corporation with thousands of employees or a small local brand. What makes the difference are people who take ownership and commit to making this Project a success. If you decide to take your Ambassador Project to the next level, we have a bonus chapter for you so that you feel informed, empowered and ready to follow the steps that will get you there faster.

Did you know that:

- Your best Ambassador might not be your CEO?
- Your colleagues might be afraid to be seen?
- If you ask one colleague to create content for other colleagues, the creator will probably leave?
- Curating content for your colleagues does not get them on board to post it?
- Using an advocacy software does not mean you have Ambassadors?

You probably have a lot on your plate already. You might feel this is a huge mountain to climb, and you do not have extra time for a project like this. We promise that the launch will be done in just 10 hours. You can have it done by the end of this week. Don't wait because those who start earlier will snatch the attention that could be yours. You are not only competing with your direct competition. You compete with anyone who targets the same clients, business partners or talent. And LinkedIn is getting more and more crowded. Let's get started and help you and your colleagues shine *right now*!

ONE
Get Your Colleagues On Board

The Project Hero said: 'I am so proud of what we are doing here, inspirational colleagues implementing great international projects, green initiatives, educating young students and graduates. We impact people's lives. That matters to me. I cannot believe I am living and breathing my values like sustainability and zero-waste in my job. LinkedIn allows me to share my work in a way that would not be possible otherwise.' We were at the board meeting, and it felt like time had just stopped. We all realised how powerful this was. That is how the Ambassador Project in dm drogerie markt, the largest retail drugstore chain in Europe started.

The world has changed forever. The heroes have taken over. Heroes who, deep within themselves, know they have something powerful to say. People love to listen to them much more than they would listen to popular company brands. Passionate individuals – company Ambassadors – are driving the world of business. Because behind every strong company, there is a hero. An ambassador.

In this chapter, we will explore:

- What buy-in is and why you need it

- What exactly the Ambassador Project is

- The benefits of the Ambassador Project

- The risks of employees using social media and how your company can manage these

- How to set and measure employee advocacy goals

What is buy-in and why do you need it?

Imagine a team of rowers, all committed to achieving their goal together, each rowing in perfect unison and harmony. Their boat effortlessly slips through the waves as they move towards success. That's the power of 'buy-in' – incredible things happen when everyone is committed to the same goal and pulling in the same direction.

When we talk about 'buy-in,' we mean getting people on board with an idea or initiative and getting them excited to participate and support it. In the case of your Ambassador Project, buy-in is crucial. We want your colleagues and key stakeholders to truly understand the potential impact this Project could have on your marketing, HR and sales efforts, and why it's a positive step forwards for your company.

When you open the topic of Employee Ambassadors, it is more than likely that your colleagues will say, 'I don't have time for another thing,' but just roll with it. Change is difficult, and even the most exciting new idea can feel like you will never be able to implement it at the beginning. But this is OK. If you show your colleagues that LinkedIn is vital and a great way to learn, share, grow and attract, they will thank you later.

We are often invited to work with companies to help them find their authentic voice when they have just signed a large contract. It may be an introverted lawyer doing their first keynote speech who asks us to help build their LinkedIn presence. Sometimes, it's when your colleagues realise that what they have to say matters to a broad audience – especially those little things about their working day. You will recognise opportunities to get buy-in when they arise. Sometimes they will thank you, sometimes they will keep it to themselves, but you will see it and never forget it.

Disengaged employees can ruin a company's reputation, prevent the engagement of other colleagues and stop others from working for you. Did you know that 69% of employees said they would work harder if they were more appreciated?[2] Company Ambassadors need to be actively supported to highlight projects, colleagues and achievements. This helps with engagement, sales, reputation, hiring and brand awareness.

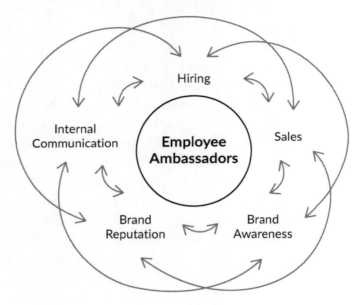

If you want to start an Ambassador Project, you need most of the company to understand why this Project matters, and why it is important. This is what internal buy-in is.

You are reading this book for a reason. Whether you see LinkedIn's limitless potential or have been given the task to finally get your LinkedIn Page moving,

---

2   Officevibe, 'Statistics on the importance of employee feedback' (1 December 2022), https://officevibe.com/blog/infographic-employee-feedback, accessed 12 September 2023

you are in the right place. We will give you an exact 10-hour plan on how to see the first results of your new LinkedIn endeavour in 30 days in a way you and your colleagues will love.

What is the Ambassador Project?

Change is coming to make companies, board members, and decision-makers more reachable. Can you feel it too? Potential clients and candidates want to hear from your employees about your company's values and how they are living them in their everyday professional lives. If you are reading this book, there is a chance you already know this.

The Ambassador Project will show you the magic of building a brand on LinkedIn through Employee Ambassadors. It is a holistic approach that touches every aspect of the employee experience, from the recruitment and onboarding process to employee development, retention, and everything in between. This way, your employees become not only promoters of your company stories, but creators of them.

What you want to achieve is a successful Ambassador Project that will run itself with decreasing intervention from you over the years. You can significantly increase the extent to which your colleagues will share information about your company or product as part of their online and social lives. That way, they also engage others and drive the changes you need.

Employee Ambassadors are selected and agree to carry the values and culture of the company to the outside world. Ambassadors use social media and other platforms to talk about their company, their colleagues, projects and tasks, and clients' results. That way, they attract new talent and customers who are ideal for the company.

You and your colleagues can be influencers that show some of your company's charm. You can use your Ambassadors in your LinkedIn army to show the world what it means to work for you and with you. They create a vivid image of your company. They convey emotions the company never could. Why? Because they live your values day in and day out. Who would you trust more – a real person that speaks to you, or the brand voice created by agencies or Artificial Intelligence (AI)?

This might seem like a steep hill to climb if you do not have your Employee Ambassadors yet, but who knows your company best? The people who work there. They understand the customers' needs and pains. For example, they know that the software developers like to play World of Warcraft every Wednesday evening. They know that Kate in the accounting department will need to hire a new part-timer next month, and that Mark in the R&D department needs detailed client feedback to improve the new product your company wants to launch.

Eighty-six per cent of employees participating in Employee Advocacy on social media, said that it positively impacted their careers.[3] Your Ambassadors need to feel honoured, recognised and joyful. Yes, joyful. Why? Because then they can write original posts that don't sound like they have been abducted by aliens. Stiff and grey LinkedIn posts will not do the heavy lifting for you and your brand. The authentic voice of that employee connects to your ideal client or potential colleague.

Pre-pandemic, clients were the most important stakeholder. Now employees have become the number one stakeholder.[4] If they really are to be recognised, they must have their voice. They must be given a chance to influence corporate strategy and publicly use their voice over social media and other platforms. Employees are no longer supporting acts; they have become the most important partner in the future of business. You need to get ready for this new era.

3   Hinge Research Institute, *Understanding Employee Advocacy on Social Media*, www.hingemarketing.com/uploads/hinge-research-employee-advocacy.pdf, accessed 25 June 2023
4   Edelman Trust Barometer 2021, *The Belief-Driven Employee*, www.edelman.com/sites/g/files/aatuss191/files/2021-08/2021Edelm anTrustBarometerSpecialReport_TheBelief-DrivenEmployee.pdf, accessed 10 May 2023

Social media platforms and Employee Ambassadors

Marketers always argue about which social media platform to use but, ultimately, you should be on all of them. Which one is the best for Employee Ambassadors (also called Employee Advocacy)? We say LinkedIn because this is our favourite platform, but we are not biased. Let's look at the facts from the Oktopost Employee Advocacy Benchmark Report:[5]

- Each social media platform works differently for Employee Ambassadors. Some social networks, like LinkedIn and Facebook, are great for facilitating deeper conversations. Others are better for quick and easy sharing, like X (formerly known as Twitter).

- LinkedIn is the most successful social media platform for B2B Employee Ambassadors. While it earned 84% fewer shares than Facebook, LinkedIn offered forty-seven times the number of link clicks generated by Facebook. Also, Employee Ambassadors' posts earned twenty-four times as many comments as Facebook and X combined.

- While X accounts for nearly 85% of all shares generated by Employee Ambassadors' posts, LinkedIn earned twelve times the engagement of

---

5   Oktopost, 2022 *Employee Advocacy Benchmark Report*, www.oktopost. com/ebooks/employee-advocacy-benchmark-report, accessed 24 February 2023

X and over seventy-four times the engagement of Facebook.

- That means that LinkedIn outperformed Facebook and X, generating over 91% of all link clicks from Employee Ambassadors' posts and accounting for nearly 95% of total conversions via employee advocacy. Conversion is what matters when it comes to return of your investment on your Ambassador Project.

Here is some interesting data to support your decision to go for an Ambassador Project:

- Having an employee advocacy programme increases the total social engagement for a brand by 25% to 40% at minimum.[6]

- Nearly half of chief marketing officers said employee advocacy was their best-performing social initiative. The next highest-performing social initiative was social selling (32%), another form of employee advocacy.[7]

- When you first talk to your sales team about Employee Ambassadors and social selling, the usual response is, 'This is not my job. That's Marketing, whereas I sell.' You can help them

---

6   ibid
7   Oktopost, *The State of B2B Social Media Marketing Report*, www. oktopost.com/ebooks/the-state-of-b2b-social-media-marketing, accessed 25 June 2023

to understand the power of social selling through numbers.

- Seventy-eight per cent of social sellers regularly outsell their less social-savvy peers.[8]

- Most of the purchase decision (83%) happens before the customer engages with a brand or its salespeople.[9]

That means that your customers know more about your company, product and employees than ever before and are looking for information through thought leadership on social media and platforms. In fact, 54% of decision-makers and 48% of C-Suite executives say they spend over an hour per day consuming thought leadership.[10]

You decide what they find and read about your company, and your colleagues can directly and authentically shape potential clients' perceptions. They show not only what your company sells, but why it matters. To them and to you. This way, you can cultivate meaningful business relationships that last. In Simon Sinek's book, *Start With Why: How Great Leaders Inspire Everyone To Take Action*, he says over

---

8   LinkedIn SSI Index, www.business.linkedin.com/sales-solutions/social-selling/the-social-selling-index-ssi-b, accessed 10 April 2023
9   Edelman Team, *2021 LinkedIn-Edelman B2B Thought Leadership Impact Report*, www.edelman.com/expertise/business-marketing/2021-b2b-thought-leadership-impact-study, accessed 10 April 2023
10 ibid

and over that: 'People do not buy what you sell, but why you sell it.'[11]

The same goes for the area of employer branding. The impact of employee advocacy is significant and measurable. Attracting talent is hard. Eighty-six per cent of HR professionals have said that recruiting is becoming more and more similar to marketing in recent years.[12]

Can you make attracting talent easier? A strong employer brand can reduce the cost of hiring by as much as 50%. In addition, those actively managing their employer brand can reduce employee turnover by as much as 28%, attract 50% more qualified applicants and hire one to two times faster.[13]

Potential employees care about your unique employer value proposition. Hint: This is not the coffee or branded mugs at your office. It's not just teamwork. It is the sense of belonging that your colleagues have. It is the authentic feeling that they are respected and cared for.

11 S Sinek, *Start With Why: How Great Leaders Inspire Everyone To Take Action* (Portfolio, 2009)

12 Glassdoor Team, 'The Most Important Employer Branding Statistics to Know' (5 April 2021), www.glassdoor.com/employers/blog/most-important-employer-branding-statistics, accessed 17 June 2023

13 LinkedIn Talent Solutions, *The Ultimate List of Employer Brand Statistics*, www.business.linkedin.com/content/dam/business/talent-solutions/global/en_us/c/pdfs/ultimate-list-of-employer-brand-stats.pdf, accessed 12 June 2023

Are you ready?

Building a brand on LinkedIn is not easy, but we promise that the cherries you pick after a few intensive hours of hard work will be sweet and juicy. LinkedIn is fun. Full of amazing inspiration with all the professional topics you can imagine. The results are also drastically different when you have a fire lit under your butt!

There is no *if* you should start to build your brand on LinkedIn. The question is, *why* do you want to do it, and are you *ready*?

Answering, 'Why now?' will help you to see if your company is ready. That is enough to start with. Refrain from thinking about the obstacles. Refrain from thinking about your colleagues who assume they have nothing to say, do not know how to make their posts attractive, or do not want to build a personal brand (just the company one). We will handle these objections in later chapters.

With the right information, you become the go-to person in your company. This is what an Ambassador Project does for you. Just imagine that you know things about other departments that other colleagues don't. How valuable would this be to you and the whole team? As a Project Hero, you will have information that can powerfully connect various departments with one vision to create a strong employer brand aligned with your company culture.

Maybe your IT department is about to deploy a new project that will transform the way you work with customer data. Or you find out the real reason why Peter, one of your key employees, decided to come back to your company after leaving it for two years for another company. If you are the Project Hero, you know magical things are happening in your company, and you can help the world to see them through your perspective.

Ninety per cent of B2B companies who really care about results will be able to drive a minimum of ten times ROI when they know what to look for. Why? Because most problems can be solved through people, networking and technology. Employee Ambassadors can get you to all of these effectively.

If your need to use Employee Ambassadors is not that important right now, and if you perceive it as 'just another task' rather than a solution to your problem in the areas of sales, hiring, reputation, internal communication and brand awareness, then revisit the idea of creating an Employee Ambassadors' Team in 6–12 months.

Do not waste time trying to solve minor problems or spend too little time solving big problems. If you need to hire one person annually, do not start a whole Ambassador Project. However, if your revenue needs to grow, you want to enter new territories or want to hire top talent consistently, then roll up your sleeves. If you see a big business reason, then you're ready. Let's go!

Risks of having Ambassadors

Having an employee speak on behalf of a company can be scary. The management team imagines the worst-case scenario of your employee commenting on a topic they should not have and causing a PR disaster.

The reality is that your employees are already on social media talking about themselves, your company, and even their work. So, you need to ensure they know how to build the company name and protect your sensitive data along the way and that they understand they aren't speaking on behalf of a company unless it is their job to do so (eg, the spokesperson).

It's worth recognising that people rely on social media when making purchasing decisions, even in the B2B context. According to a study by IDC (Social Buying Meets Social Selling), 84% of C-Suite executives and 70% of B2B decision-makers use social media to inform their purchase choices. Looking ahead, it is predicted that by 2026, a significant portion of Millennial and Gen Z consumers – around 60% – will prefer making purchases on social platforms rather than traditional, digital commerce platforms. This highlights the growing significance of social media in the consumer landscape (B2C) and reinforces the importance of leveraging it effectively for business purposes.[14]

---

14   J Turner, 'The Top 6 Marketing Predictions for 2022', Gartner (10 January 2022), www.gartner.com/en/marketing/insights/articles/the-top-6-marketing-predictions-for-2022, accessed 5 May 2023

Do you know what potential clients and candidates do when they want to apply for a job? They stalk. Your social media and your employees' profiles can determine if they will send you their LinkedIn profile or a CV.

Make it easy for them to find relevant colleagues who know how important their LinkedIn activity is and how to show their expertise, values and personality to attract new members of the team and clients.

B2B business is not transactional. It is about relation-ships, and every great salesman will know that. With your company Ambassadors in place, your company reach is at least ten times higher. With their input, you will get to a new audience and people you could never reach as a company.

So, what happens if your employees become active on LinkedIn and start to get job offers? Chances are they are already getting offers on LinkedIn, but they are not building your brand along the way. What do you think will happen if they build only their personal brand? With our background as head-hunters, we can reassure you that a person that is satisfied in their job will not leave, and if they are not satisfied, they will leave anyway.

In our experience, the risk of having your colleagues on social media without knowing what to post and, most importantly, what not to post, is far more dangerous than proactively empowering them to build their personal brands along with the company brand. They will talk about your company anyway; with the right Employee Ambassadors, you get to influence what information goes out and how your target audience receives it. When your employee is invited to talk about the current trends at a conference, they will convey the exact message you want to be told. Why? Because they have seen their boss on LinkedIn, posting about the vital elements of the company's brand, culture and what you stand for.

With Employee Ambassadors, the mission poster on your wall becomes a real experience ingrained in the company's DNA.

Safeguarding your company's reputation

The concern that an employee might tarnish a company's reputation with a single thoughtless post is valid. Some of the actions can even have legal consequences. In the digital world, employees have an unprecedented level of influence. Social media is flooded with unfiltered views and experiences of employees. Let's explore the incredible role of Employee Ambassadors in mitigating reputational risks for your company.

Global communication firm Weber Shandwick's survey, covering fifteen countries and organisations with over 500 employees, provides insightful data supporting this shift. Nearly six in ten respondents have already defended their employer – within private circles and publicly. Employees are stepping up to support organisations in times of need. This trend emphasises the rise of a new genre of employee activism – one that you can harness to safeguard and enhance your company's reputation.[15]

Employee Ambassadors have a unique ability to shield your company's reputation from the negative impact of damaging posts. They act as a robust line of defence, leveraging their networks and credibility to swiftly respond, engage, and disseminate positive content that counters the harmful narrative.

This transformative movement opens up new opportunities for you, and your Employee Ambassadors are at the heart of it. Your visible colleagues are role models embodying your company's core values and ideals. They are the faces of your brand, the human touch behind the business, and the ones who breathe life into your company's story. That way, they can strategically influence clients, potential talent, and media perception, shaping and preserving your company's reputation.

---

15 Weber Shandwick, *Employees Rising: Seizing the Opportunity in Employee Activism*, www.webershandwick.com/uploads/news/files/employees-rising-seizing-the-opportunity-in-employee-activism.pdf, accessed 22 August 2023

Selecting the right Employee Ambassadors lets you turn potential reputational risks into opportunities. Your Ambassador Team can safeguard your reputation by:

- Amplifying positive information: They share success stories, industry insights, and thought leadership content showcasing your company's best aspects. This proactive approach creates a reservoir of goodwill. In addition, it makes it easier to counteract any negative narratives that may arise.

- Building trust and credibility: By actively engaging with their networks, these Ambassadors establish themselves as trustworthy sources of information, creating a ripple effect that extends to their connections. This network of individuals is more likely to believe and support positive messaging about your company, strengthening its reputation.

- Creating advocates outside the company: Seeing employees' enthusiasm and dedication for months or years also builds a community of clients, media and other supporters who are ready to step up in times of need.

- Giving a swift response when a damaging post occurs: The Ambassador Team steps up, leveraging their extensive connections and trusted relationships. As a result, they can rapidly address the issue, share accurate information, correct misconceptions and provide an authentic perspective.

Setting the Project goals and measuring results

Close your eyes and think about your company. What is the first thing that comes to your mind?

You might think of your innovative products, excellent customer service, great colleagues, passionate leadership team, successful business model, strong brand or significant revenue.

Now think again. What are the challenges your company faces?

Pressure to increase sales, lack of talent in significant roles, retiring colleagues who will influence your business significantly in the upcoming years, salespeople who lack drive, are settled, don't want to try new things, aggressive competition with better distribution. Maybe even former employees are trolling you on your social media.

Download the playsheets here and use them for the action steps throughout this book. Let the journey begin!

✎ ACTION STEP

Working through the table, think about your company's pros and cons.

	Pros in your company	Cons in your company
Hiring		
Sales		
Brand awareness		
Reputation risk		
Internal communication		

From our experience, the majority of employees (around 60%) are willing to share some company news and information on social media from time to time. However only a small percentage actually do because of unclear goals, systems and guidelines, lack of training, and fear of negative consequences. When you decide to step up your game, you will unleash the full potential of your Employee Ambassadors. Let's start with setting up the right goals.

If you do not know where you are driving to, the chances of you getting there are pretty low. You want to work on projects that bring massive value to you as a person and your company. How do you ensure that your goals are challenging, but reachable? Simplify this by choosing one area and sticking to it. Other areas will be taken care of by the individual Ambassadors and their goals discussed in later chapters.

✎ ACTION STEP

Which of the following will be your priority over the next 12 months?

- Increased revenue and/or profit
- Hiring of new talent
- Retaining talent/increasing employee engagement
- Being visible as a leader in your industry
- Reputation damage control (collective redundancy, etc)

Each Ambassador Project measures different metrics according to the Project goal. Here are some of the metrics to start with:

- Number of connections vs followers on personal profiles

- Profile views, search appearances

- The number and structure of followers, and their behaviour patterns on the LinkedIn Company Page (officially known as LinkedIn Page)

- Number of posts and their engagement

- Social Selling Index (SSI) of the management and Ambassadors

- Number of leads, media outlets, candidates

- Employee attrition and turnover

- Conversion during in-person/online meetings with clients, candidates, potential business partners and many more

- Google Analytics – behaviour patterns of visitors from LinkedIn

- LinkedIn Ads, retargeting, etc

- Social listening tools

- Awards received per ambassador/company

- Marketing attribution reports

- Revenue growth

- Revenue per client

- Profit margin

- Client retention rate

- Branded search volume

- Calculated media value

You do not want a weak target, but measuring what your colleagues cannot influence makes them demotivated and want to disappear. You want a motivated army of colleagues with you. Do not worry. No one is alone in an Ambassador Project. You have them, and you have us.

Start with your Project goal and then reverse engineer the metrics that make sense to measure. Of course, the main metrics are always directly connected to the primary goal. If your brand is well known, you probably have an advantage budget wise, but from our experience, even the companies with a well-known brand want to speak about products/services other than what they are known for. For example, a B2C company intends to support hiring IT specialists, a B2B tax consultancy wants to rebrand as the number one choice for green economy experts, etc. LinkedIn is a different world.

What are the most critical metrics to be measured? The ones that will show you the exact amount of progress made towards your Number One Ambassador Project goal. If you need it, get help from a colleague who loves to dig into data. Together, you can spot trends easily, measure content and engagement impact, and make informed decisions to keep the Project on the right track.

You are the visionary. We want you to be ready to connect the dots and draw the things others cannot see.

Once your colleagues see the opportunities, they will be hooked. Once they want to know more, you can move to the next step: selecting your Ambassadors.

Summary

In this chapter we have covered:

- What internal buy-in is, and why you need it for your Project to succeed
- The five elements of LinkedIn as the solution to multiple business challenges
- What the Ambassador Project is
- Social media platforms and different uses according to your goals
- Risks of having Employee Ambassadors
- Setting goals and measuring results

TWO
Ambassador Volunteers

If you are reading this book, you know you are missing opportunities on LinkedIn. You may have tried
to use LinkedIn yourself or have helped some of your
colleagues to start building your company brand. You
have motivated them to share company content. They
have done workshops on LinkedIn, and maybe you
have bought expensive software to make sharing on
social media easy for them. Maybe they even posted
for a while, but then... Nada. Their motivation is
gone, and they have lost momentum. This is not your
fault. It happens often.

The task is clear. They need to go on LinkedIn and
post about how they love their work, their clients and
their colleagues so that they attract other people who
are similar and who you would love to work with.

You want them to ramp up their LinkedIn game and build your company brand on LinkedIn simultaneously to increase revenue and attract top talent.

You do your best, but other business priorities, Key Performance Indicators (KPIs), projects, kids, pets, you name it, continue to get in the way. You believe there has to be a better way to do this quickly and simply. Starting the Ambassador Project will help you do this.

Should you turn every employee into an Ambassador? You do not have to, and we do not advise you to do so. Glassdoor.com is full of reviews of how companies force their employees to praise them and engage with company content. If you do this, they will share this information privately, or worse, on various platforms and social media. This is definitely not the way you want to approach it. Respect the integrity of personal brands and only work with colleagues who want to participate.

Let's start by defining the four key roles of the Ambassador Team. Having the right people in the right places is the key to success.

The four roles of the Ambassador Project

You need four roles to create a successful Ambassador Project: Ambassadors, Cheerleaders, the Project Hero and the Project Guardian. Every role has its own purpose, activities and challenges. However, if you are a small company, these roles can be merged.

The roles of Project Hero and Project Guardian are given to people who care about starting the Ambassador Project. You may already have one of these two roles. Once you have the Project Hero and the Project Guardian roles defined, you need to focus on your Ambassadors.

The Project Guardian

The Ambassador Project is a top to bottom activity. Without management actively participating, it will be difficult. If the CEO says, 'I don't like social media, go and do it for me,' or, 'I don't see how this could be useful,' there's little chance that your colleagues will be fired up to be your company voice. Why would they? They need to feel trusted, supported and recognised for their efforts.

Your Project Guardian is anyone in your leadership team who is strongly rooting for you and can approve the budget for your Ambassador Project. For example, the CEO, a member of the board or a director. Do you have a Project Guardian in your management team?

❑ Not yet? Go back to Chapter 1 and share some data and examples to support the need of

Employee Ambassadors with your management team.

❏ Yes? Great. Read on.

Project Guardians need to powerfully communicate how important the voices of their Ambassadors are. If they create content – amazing! Even if they don't, their support is like water to a mill. Whether it is an occasional comment in reply to their posts, a tap on the back in the elevator saying, 'I saw your post. You're doing a great job,' or a couple of sentences about a particular Ambassador during a critical meeting, this support does wonders and changes the whole trajectory of the Project.

The Project Hero

In every project, you need someone who takes ownership for the Ambassador Project: the KPIs, the delegation of tasks, implementation and overall atmosphere in the team. This role is both rewarding and tough. The Project Hero needs to be prepared to pull the team towards their goals and deal with the pushback that will undoubtedly come. Usually this is a mid-senior or senior level employee in the marketing, PR, internal communications or HR department.

The Project Hero is responsible for choosing the right Ambassadors. Unfortunately, a bad choice means bad results. Later in this chapter, you will find guidance on choosing the right people to reach your Number One goal.

We will also provide you with our 10-hour Launch Plan later in this book so, as the Project Hero, you need to be organised. We are looking for a cheerful personality that can be tough when necessary. Are you the Project Hero? If the answer is 'no', do you know a perfect Project Hero?

The Ambassador

Employees know the company best. They are a trusted source of information about the company, its culture, employees, values, products or vacancies. Every Employee Ambassadors Project is based on the Ambassador role.

Ambassadors create their own content with their own opinions and ideas. They have project KPIs and need at least an hour a week or, depending on the goal, two to three hours to dedicate to LinkedIn activities. These are not extra hours – they replace other activities with social engagement. Employee advocacy will save every department in the organisation a lot of time in the long run and they need to believe and feel that this Project is important for your company's success.

If you are concerned about whether you will find a group of people who would be willing to become

Employee Ambassadors for your brand, our client Generali had the same worries. They managed to successfully find a committed group from different levels of management and from various departments. A board member even volunteered to get involved in the Project, which is unusual. Their Ambassador Project meetings 'felt like a reward'.

Thanks to the Project, Generali enhanced their brand on LinkedIn locally and even on an international level. Local content has been used in material posted on social media channels by the main group.

Ambassadors need to be active for at least a year because you want your Ambassadors to be recognisable and easily identified with your company. LinkedIn followers need some time to get used to this. When you set this boundary, you also protect your time and financial investment in educating and taking care of your Ambassadors. The Project Hero needs to keep up with their Ambassadors' activities and motivate them during this period. If you choose too many Ambassadors, the responsibility will be dispersed. We'll come to this later in the chapter. In the case of Ambassadors, less is always more. Being an Ambassador is a reward. If you have too many volunteers for this role, let them know you only have five places available. If they are active on LinkedIn, you can add them in the next round.

> **TOP TIP**
>
> In some companies, one colleague will create content for all the Ambassadors. This is not sustainable. Your LinkedIn will not be as successful as it could be taking this approach and you may lose this one person because it is exhausting.

The Cheerleader

Everyone in your company can be a Cheerleader. Whether online or offline, they come up with ideas for content for all other team roles and for the Company Page. They engage with the posts and know their support makes all the difference.

According to LinkedIn, 30% of Company Page engagement comes from its own employees. These employees are fourteen times more likely to share their employer's content compared to other content types.[16] It may seem strange to only get comments from colleagues, but what is stranger is when even employees are not reacting. Sometimes we see colleagues in a conversation about an important topic. The exchange happens on LinkedIn and is public. This is great because clients and potential colleagues see what it is like to work for your company.

---

16   R Jobanputra, 'LinkedIn Pages and Elevate — better together' (1 January 2021), LinkedIn Ads Blog, www.linkedin.com/business/ marketing/blog/linkedin-pages/linkedin-pages-and-elevate-better-together, accessed 9 September 2023

Give your Cheerleaders training and information about your social media policies to protect both your brand name and to protect your colleagues from the risks of being visible online.

The table on the next page gives an overview of who the best type of people for each of the four project roles are, their purpose, and their activities.

You do not have to be a huge international company to make an impact on LinkedIn. Your project roles can be merged depending on your company struc-ture. If you are an owner of a small company and you are the only Ambassador in your Ambassador Project at the beginning, your employees can be your Cheerleaders. They do not have to create content; they just need to support yours. It will take them less than 10 minutes a week. Showing them your results can motivate them to start their own adventure as Ambassadors.

If you are a solo entrepreneur, you will need to find your Cheerleaders outside your company. Be innova-tive. Create a support group. Surround yourself with people who care about you and your business and help each other with support on LinkedIn.

	The Project Guardian	The Project Hero	The Ambassadors	The Cheerleaders
Purpose	• Leading by example • Approving the budget • Showing the team this project is important	• Project ownership • Leading by example • Setting and checking KPIs • Delegating project tasks • Responsibility for the implementation • Knowledge transfer • Team motivation	• Carrier of information • Content creator • Responsibility for own and project KPIs	• Helping others to share their thoughts • Supporting project team online and offline
Activities	• Engaging with company and ambassador content • Comments, likes, re-posts • Occasional content	• Goal setting • Creating and implementing strategy • Arranging regular meetings • Checking KPIs	• Regular content creation • Meeting the KPIs • Adding new relevant connections	• Engaging with company and team members' content

	The Project Guardian	The Project Hero	The Ambassadors	The Cheerleaders
		• Answering team's questions • Content creation • Engaging with company and ambassador content	• Engaging with company and team members' content	• Coming up with content ideas relevant to their departments and teams
Best person for this role	• Top manager, board member • Open to new ideas, visionary, likes technology, charismatic, adds spark into the team.	• Senior level, action-taker from Marketing, Sales, HR or Product Dept • Positive personality, likes project ownership, sees the potential of Ambassadors • Prepared to be celebrated, but ready to get through the pushback	• Senior level employee • Willing to share and be visible, feels project ownership, responsible, has a problem that needs to be solved	• Everyone in the company who does not have any of the previous three roles

Attributes				
• Is on the same page as The Hero • Has a high-quality LinkedIn personal profile • Attends Ambassador meetings occasionally to show support	• Chooses the right Ambassadors • Is motivated and energised • Understands the results can be magical • Commits to the project fully	• Know their responsibilities and the activities they have to do regularly • Are ready to commit to the project for at least 6 months • Have a branded profile (not a CV), and know that they represent the company, not just themselves	• Know why the project needs to start now • Know the benefits it brings to them personally and to the company • Have basic tech knowledge to support other team members • Have good personal profiles with your brand in their headlines

Managing expectations

The Project Hero will choose the priorities for the next 12 months in the first Action Step (Chapter 1). First, focus on your company goal. We want to set you up for success, so start small. Even if you have thousands of colleagues, begin with a small ambassador team.

From our experience, five Ambassadors work best. In some cases, up to nine is OK, but it costs the Project Hero to look after more people. Five is big enough to create a buzz, but small enough to take ownership and feel they belong. With five Ambassadors, you can get amazing results. You might get a call from a CEO of a company you have been trying to sell to for years. You might fill a vacancy within a matter of days. Even better, your company could be named Employer of the Year. All of this has happened to our clients, thanks to their Ambassador Project.

If you are a small company, you can create your own magic, too. Remember, you only need two to three active people to double your revenue. The real Ambassador Project is about people. It is an honest, two-way cooperation between you and your coworkers, so you don't need to buy fancy software to prepare and share your posts at the beginning.

In Chapter 6, we will give the 10-hour plan to set up your first Employee Ambassador pilot. When you implement it, you will see the first results in just 30 days, but don't expect to have your whole organisation cheering you on LinkedIn. It will take time. Generally, getting confident on LinkedIn takes people three to six months. The bigger the company, the longer it takes.

Just start with small steps. When your coworkers see the results, you'll have them on board.

The unique Ambassador's adventure

'I hated LinkedIn. My feed was full of weird posts that didn't interest me and I was afraid to view other people's profiles. I didn't want to be seen as a stalker. Then I became an Ambassador. Now, I love it. LinkedIn is a network where hatred is absent, discussions are classy, and people are kind and inspiring. And I became one of the Top 20 Best Marketers on LinkedIn in our country,' said our client Katarina Kretter, the Project Hero from company ENVI-PAK.

Katarina shed light on the love-hate relationship that people often have with LinkedIn. By changing her thinking, she ignited a new wave of interest within the entire company for leveraging the platform. This momentum gained further traction as Ambassadors from various departments, including the CEO, rallied behind her. As a result, the company witnessed a significant increase in followers on their LinkedIn Page, surpassing six-fold growth. Not only did they become highly visible as the leading Producer Responsibility

Organisation locally, but they also gained international visibility from other stakeholders.

Every Ambassador is unique and will have their own unique adventure. Each one of them will have their own KPIs. You will have colleagues from different departments with goals like:

- Increasing sales, revenue and/or profit
- Hiring new talent/increasing candidate conversion during interviews
- Retaining talent/increasing employee engagement
- Being visible as a thought leader in your niche and industry
- Winning an award for the company/Ambassador and/or the team

The company goal you set in Chapter 1 covers every role: Guardian, Hero, Ambassador and Cheerleader. Every person in the team has their own goal. Getting them going will be much harder if the goal is not big enough or important enough. We will talk about selecting the right Ambassadors later in this chapter.

If you have colleagues whose work problems keep them awake at night, they might be the perfect Ambassadors. The reason is simple. They feel it in their guts, so they really need to find a solution.

Promoting the Ambassador role

Being a company Ambassador is an honour. Sell it this way. It is not a chore; it's not something else 'to be done'. Embracing the Ambassador role opens doors to unparalleled experiences and growth – opportunities your colleagues would never be exposed to if they were not part of the team.

Social media content shared by employees has eight times more engagement than content shared through the company's own social channels and is shared twenty-five times more frequently.[17]

What's in it for me, aka the 'WIIFM factor', is one of the keys. If you show your colleagues that you know what their pain is and how Employee Ambassadors will help them solve it, they start to listen. Then you can tell them what is in it for the company and how this synergically supports their personal brand.

Ninety-eight per cent of employees use at least one social media site for personal use, of which 50% are already posting about their company.[18] Why not help them to build their professional and company brand

---

17   M Biro, 'How to Create a Social Media Advocacy', *Entrepreneur* (7 December 2016), www.entrepreneur.com/science-technology/how-to-create-a-social-media-advocacy-program/285613, accessed 15 June 2023

18   T Kunsman, 'Eye-Popping Employee Advocacy Statistics That Matter the Most', EveryoneSocial (10 January 2023), https://everyonesocial.com/blog/employee-advocacy-statistics, accessed 23 June 2023

along the way? The better the company's employer brand, the better people it will attract and the better they look working for you.

Ambassadors will also get training, support and an accountability group to build their thought leadership position in record time. This would usually take them a long time and sometimes they may never even start.

People need to understand how being an Ambassador directly reinforces their professional positioning. They will have access to information and people from other departments on a project strongly supported by the management. This makes them more valuable to the company and brings them opportunities from within the company. They become known outside your company and receive requests to talk to media, podcasters or at conferences. They get known as the most influential people in their niche. They attract fantastic talent to their teams and departments and find solutions no one ever thought of because of their high-quality professional networking.

Ask your colleagues: 'We are about to enhance our brand in a new and exciting way. Will you join us?'

How to select Ambassadors

Talk to those who have decided to join in the Project or ask them to answer a short survey. You need information on how active they are on social media and if they understand the commitment to post.

Sometimes we are asked if it is OK for an Ambassador to switch to the role of a Cheerleader. No, it is not. Ambassadors commit to 12 months of content creation. Losing one of them will demotivate the whole team. Be transparent about your expectations and their KPIs right from the start.

Ambassadors must be willing to connect with strangers. Gaining traction for their content will be much harder with only a couple of hundred connections. Usually, we aim for 1,500 or more. If you're curious about the potential for gaining new followers on LinkedIn, allow us to share two success stories of our clients.

Monika Petlušová, Manager of European Union Initiative EPALE in Slovakia, aimed to share the impressive projects that EPALE creates. Over the course of one and half years, she expanded her network from 127 connections to an impressive 6,700 strategically chosen and relevant contacts. Today, she enjoys connections with influential individuals across the European Union, opening doors to valuable opportunities like speaking at renowned conferences abroad. Through her strategic LinkedIn activities, she has successfully elevated the visibility of EPALE and established herself as a respected thought leader.

Andrej Viceník is the Chief Corporate Officer and member of the Board of Directors at VÚB banka (Intesa Sanpaolo Group). Initially armed with just over 1,000 followers, and with a sporadic presence, Andrej embarked on a two-year journey fuelled by strategic activities, unwavering dedication, and the power of his own voice. Andrej's professional network flourished, expanding organically to 30,000 followers all keen to interact with the thoughts, ideas, and experiences he shares with an authentic touch of humour. His remarkable growth on LinkedIn showcases the exciting possibilities that can be achieved with a well-defined strategy and a commitment to fostering meaningful connections and creating authentic content.

Do not choose the Ambassadors for your leadership team if they are not ready to post regularly. They can be either Project Guardians or Cheerleaders instead. Nothing depletes the team like losing team members on the way.

TOP TIP

The Ambassadors do not have to be from management. With spark and passion, your colleagues in less senior roles can create much more buzz around your company.

Who makes a perfect Ambassador? When creating the Ambassador Team, members should meet all of the below criteria.

Your Perfect Ambassador

- Is passionate about the company
- Posts at least once a week
- Invests 1 or 2 hours per week on LinkedIn
- Increases the number of followers consistently
- Regularly meets with the team

Content guidelines for Ambassadors

Think about the consequences when a frustrated employee vents on LinkedIn or a team member unintentionally shares sensitive information in a conference photo. Now, imagine a different scenario – those same employees, empowered with the right knowledge and guidance, sharing positive experiences and valuable insights that enhance your company's reputation and appeal to clients and top talent.

In the midst of potential harm, whether intentional or not, having a well-structured Ambassador Project goes beyond being a smart strategy. It becomes a crucial part of your company's brand management, safeguarding its image and ensuring responsible online presence.

If you want active and engaged Employee Ambassadors, it's time to provide structured content guidelines and let go of excessive control. Censoring their content will only lead to disengagement, and you can expect them to stop posting within 3 months. Trust your Ambassadors. Choose individuals who are not only enthusiastic, but also align with your brand values and have a genuine passion for representing your organisation.

By granting your Ambassadors the autonomy to share their unique perspectives and experiences, you empower them to become authentic advocates for your brand. This level of trust encourages their active participation and nurtures a sense of ownership and pride in their role as company Ambassadors.

Successful Ambassador Projects are built on trust, mutual respect and the freedom to express oneself. By embracing these principles, you'll create an environment where your Ambassadors thrive, making a meaningful impact on your company's LinkedIn presence.

Some of the specific cases you want to address in your social media guidelines are:

- **The unwitting exposure.** Picture an enthusiastic employee at an internal conference, capturing a group photo for a LinkedIn post. Unknowingly, sensitive client information on a background whiteboard slips into the shot.

- **The detonated departure.** Viral quitting is not a new trend. Employees use live or prepared social media posts as unique resignation letters. Some of these posts go viral. One example is 'An Interpretive Dance For My Boss Set To Kanye West's Gone' by Marina Shifrin, which has 19 million views to date.[19] Even senior executives rant in LinkedIn posts, making their exits viral. Your social media guidelines can guide employees to express their concerns internally, thus avoiding a public spectacle.

- **The cultural misfire.** Show your colleagues how to de-escalate a social media storm if an employee posts a seemingly harmless joke on LinkedIn, unaware of its offensive undertones to particular communities. Your social media guidelines should prevent this from happening, but if it does, they need to know they have to contact your PR department (in large companies) or director (in small companies) immediately.

- **The privacy intrusion.** Think of an employee sharing a casual team gathering photo on LinkedIn, unintentionally infringing on a colleague's privacy. This accidental overstep can spark questions about your company's respect for personal boundaries. A structured Ambassador Project can foster a deeper understanding of

---

19 M Shifrin, 'An Interpretive Dance For My Boss Set To Kanye West's "Gone"' (28 September 2013), www.youtube.com/watch?v=Ew_tdY0V4Zo&ab_channel=MarinaShifrin, accessed 15 April 2023

privacy considerations, reinforcing trust among your team, clients and customers.

- **The values disconnect.** Amidst a heated LinkedIn debate, an employee's communication aggressively contradicts your company's values of open dialogue and collaboration. Let your Employee Ambassadors know they are the torchbearers of your company values. Show them how to provide constructive feedback and engage in thoughtful conversation instead of resorting to aggression or offensive language.

- **Dealing with 'haters.'** If you want to make natural waves and build thought leaders in your niche, your Ambassadors need to use their creative expression to show what it means to work for you. Give them guidelines and support them if something goes wrong. It's natural that they may be criticised when they express opinions. They will have haters (and if they don't, then they are playing it too safe). Give them the confidence and the tools they'll need to handle these people graciously.

Your guidelines will depend on your industry, but start with:

- Using and posting pictures (confidential info reveal, GDPR, intellectual property)

- How to work with approved logos, taglines, hashtags, curated content and company descriptions

- Talking about competitors and clients and supporting their content

- Dealing with negative or harmful comments

- How to handle spammers and date invitations

We have covered the foundational topics for your Ambassadors' guidelines. Now you need to customise the guidelines to fit your company's specific needs and culture. By providing comprehensive but clear guidelines, you empower your Ambassadors to handle the majority of situations independently. This approach ensures that their actions align with your company's values and desired image. When employees feel empowered and supported, they are more likely to make informed decisions that positively represent your brand.

How to manage those not selected

You can have many more volunteers than you have available Ambassador roles. That is a good sign. Tell your colleagues why they have not been chosen for the Ambassador Project. Maybe they have too few followers, or they've been lurking around social media for years but never posting their opinions. Perhaps they are unable to commit to 12 months of being an Ambassador.

That is OK. Those not selected should still have a chance to attend LinkedIn training, become active and show interest. Talk to them again if you see them posting for a month or two regularly. You may add a new Ambassador for the launch, or they may become the first Ambassador for the next round.

When you communicate this transparently and positively, you will have a dedicated Cheerleader, and even a potential Ambassador for the future. Getting the chance to be an Ambassador is a reward for those who work for it.

Summary

Now you know:

- The specifics of each role you need in your Ambassador Project: Ambassadors, Cheerleaders, Project Hero and Project Guardian – each have a different purpose and activities

- What to expect and how to manage your and the team's expectations and align their Project goals with the Number One company goal

- How to choose the people who best fit the four project roles

- What it takes to be an Ambassador and their unique path

- How employees can volunteer for these roles and what opportunities are waiting for them

- How to protect company information and your colleagues through social media guidelines

- How to reframe the Project for those not selected as Ambassadors

THREE

Content Creation Is Full Of Opportunities

'How do we create content that converts? When should we post it?' It's funny how almost all of our business conversations start with these questions. It's like when Stephen King is asked time and again which pen he uses to write with. It doesn't matter. What's more important is to know *why* you want to share a thought – why should it matter to your audience, and why does it matter to you?

In this chapter we will cover what content creation is, the top ten challenges companies have when creating content, and solutions to those challenges. You will also find out why you need evergreen content and how to create it.

What is content creation?

You have the power to control your brand reputation, change opinions and inspire others to join your company or cause by simply using your phone. Would you dare to do that? Will you help your colleagues to tap into the world of content creation?

Ten years ago, we heard that everyone would have a chance to become a channel of information in the future. We could not believe it. Regular people using their social media platforms to share their opinions, ideas and lives? In their own studios, streaming from work or home? It seemed highly improbable, especially in business. But here we are today: the attention economy. Individuals on social media are having greater reach than traditional media like CNN, who have thousands of employees. Content consumers become content creators and spend their time more efficiently, have an impact on levels they would never have imagined and build strong personal and company brands on the way. You can do it, too.

Content creation means sharing information which is important to you as a company and/or as a person to create a specific image in a way that helps you to reach your business and personal goals. But there are challenges in creating content. Having worked with content creators for over a decade, we have identified their biggest fears and challenges. The issues of most companies and individuals are surprisingly similar. The difference is how they deal with them.

Top ten content challenges and solutions

Every problem has a solution. If you or your team struggle with any of these reasons not to post, we have the solutions:

Challenge 1: Posts on LinkedIn need to be professional

Is the content professional enough? If your team are asking themselves this question, we assure you that their content will be professional. There is a more important question that they should be asking at this point, however.

Solution

First ask yourself, 'How can I make my content more human?' and then, 'How can I make my content more like me?' Authenticity wins the hearts of your followers. Your audience will show you what they like and what they don't. Trust them. They are guiding you with their own engagement.

Challenge 2: We don't have time for this

Creating a piece of content can take you 3 hours or 10 minutes depending on your preparation, knowledge, skill, process and mindset. Do not assume that people will notice or appreciate a piece of content because you have spent hours writing it. The things they care about are:

- Is this new information or does it add a new perspective?

- Does it inspire me to feel or do something?

- Does it help me to save time/money?

- Does this entertain me?

Solution

We always make sure that the Ambassador Project saves time at the end of the day. It does not mean adding something. It means replacing other activities for a more effective one. If it was strategically written, with your Lead and goal in mind, then a snappy post created in 10 minutes may bring more clients than a 3,000-word article. You defined your goal in Chapter 1. We will go deeper into understanding who you are writing for (your Lead) in Chapter 4. Invest time in these top three ways to create content faster.

1. Have a structured system so that you and your colleagues can capture content ideas (eg, text/pictures/video).

2. Build an accountability structure that makes posting habitual for you and the whole team.

3. Have a system to repurpose content and do not waste something you already created.

Challenge 3: We don't know what to post about

Your potential clients and colleagues do not think about your content as much as you do. That sets you free to experiment, fail, try new things, succeed and do it all over again. Don't use what is on your company website. Let your followers feel like insiders in your company. Let them have access to premium information.

Solution

These are ten content ideas you can use right away for your Company Page:

1. Leadership and company culture

2. Career success stories of our employees

3. Projects we are working on and why they matter to us

4. Myths about our industry

5. Our innovations

6. Our products and services presented through stories

7. How we create our products

8. Client testimonials

9. Fun facts and trivia about our company/ industry/colleagues/departments

10. Awards/certifications we have and why they are important for our clients

These are ten content ideas you can use for your personal profile:

1. Little quirks I have that make me unique

2. How to save time/money in our niche/position

3. What are the trends I see for the future?

4. Technology I like to use and why

5. How my hobbies help me focus/be creative/ resilient at work

6. How does it feel to work for our company?

7. Documenting business trips

8. Lessons learned in personal and/or business life.

9. Causes I care about

10. Asking for help (ideas, marketing research, product feedback)

✏ ACTION STEP

Take a moment to think about some of your team's biggest work challenges. Take a moment to write down six topics in your notebook that you would like to talk about: three for your personal profile and three for the Company Page.

Challenge 4: Our employees don't feel confident posting

If your future Ambassadors do not feel confident posting, then let them be Cheerleaders. Ambassadors are here to create content and build company reputation along the way.

Solution

In Chapter 2 you discovered how to choose the right Ambassadors. If you choose them correctly, give them training and continuous support, they will become confident with time. If your Ambassadors need more support, ask them why they do not feel confident:

- Are they afraid that they will be too personal? Teach them that they can be personable without discussing private matters. There is a big difference between both.

- Are they afraid of haters? Make sure they are properly trained in how to deal with and respond to them.

- Do they feel pushed by the company to post, even if they do not want to? Don't push them. Ever. This can only backfire. Go back to Chapter 1 for buy-in tips.

- Are they afraid to be seen? Everyone suffers with imposter syndrome, whether they admit it or not. Interestingly, the more expert you are, the higher the chance that you will feel unqualified to talk about your topic.

- Do they feel controlled and are they afraid to overshare? Use company social media policies and proper training to help them.

Discuss these challenges openly. There is no challenge you cannot solve as a team when you work together to fit the personal and business goals you have set in Chapter 1.

Challenge 5: Our colleagues have stopped posting

A colleague posting here and there a few times a year is not an Ambassador. Employee advocacy does not mean random acts of social. In this book you will find many tips on how to deal with the reasons Ambassadors usually quit and what to do about it. Here are six major reasons why your Ambassadors stop posting.

1. They do not have a formal, structured system to follow.

2. They do not see it as a company priority.

3. They do not feel valued.

4. They feel controlled.

5. They lose inspiration.

6. They do not see the engagement they desire.

You want your team to create the perfect content, but there is one thing you need to know. There is no such thing as perfect content. It does not have to be perfect. Content creation is about continuous growth – you grow as your audience grows. Your first draft and your first posts might be time-consuming and under-performing, but that is OK.

If you do not post, you are safe. No one can criticise you. But if you take the chance, just think about how your life could change by being more visible.

Solution

Follow our 10-hour Launch Plan. You will find all of the steps in Chapter 6 of this book. Ensure your Ambassadors understand the goals, KPIs and the exact steps they need to take to be sustainably success-ful on social media.

Challenge 6: What if no one likes our posts?

If you decide to be safe and share only company products or services, open positions and catalogues, your content may lack spark. There will be the same lack of spark if you just copy the exact information from your website. Your audience is not going to be interested in that. This type of content is easily interchangeable. Be unapologetically yourself. Be authentic and write as you speak. It helps your audience to fall in love with your passion.

Solution

The good news is that this will never happen if you have a formal Ambassador Project in place. Your colleagues will know why and how to support you from the beginning. Remember, according to LinkedIn, 30% of engagement on Company Pages comes from their own employees.[20] It pleases the LinkedIn algorithm, ensures more engagement and helps your Company Page admins, too.

Your company's visual identity is the best way to be recognisable, but don't go overboard with branding. Let your Ambassadors have some fun and produce content from their own perspective – especially

---

20 R Jobanputra, 'LinkedIn Pages and Elevate — better together' (1 January 2021), LinkedIn Ads Blog, www.linkedin.com/business/marketing/blog/linkedin-pages/linkedin-pages-and-elevate-better-together, accessed 9 September 2023

images. It allows your followers see your company in brand new ways while remembering they're viewing something produced within an internal team. This maximises relevance and authenticity for your followers who experience more than just posts that seem generic.

Challenge 7: What if we succeed and spend whole days on social media?

There is a difference between being a consumer of social media vs being a creator. The social media consumer spends, on average, 2 hours and 31 minutes a day mindlessly scrolling through social media without any particular purpose.[21]

Content creators know why they use social media, what the benefits are and how to reach personal and company goals with the least time on social media. Content creators bring value to others, support company reputation and change lives on the way.

Solution

Turn your colleagues, who are regular social media consumers, into creators. They will save hours of time and will turn it to an investment in their future.

---

21 R Moody, 'Screen Time Statistics: Average Screen Time in US vs. the rest of the world' (15 March 2023), www.comparitech.com/tv-streaming/screen-time-statistics, accessed 9 September 2023

Challenge 8: What do we do with haters?

Having your own hater is a good thing. It means your content was so popular, that it reached outside your circle of closest connections and was worthy of reaction. There are two types of unpleasant conversations. You may meet a notorious hater that everyone knows, or you may experience criticism, some of which may be constructive.

Responding to the critic can become your next post, like one follower who wrote under our post: 'You encourage personal posts, but then LinkedIn becomes Facebook.' We used this comment as a prompt for our next post. The result? We tagged her, and she responded that she was proud to be a resource for our content. Now she understands that she can write about creating her artworks during weekends along with the professional content about her current projects. Her audience likes it, too. What seemed like a negative comment was actually genuine curiosity.

Solution

Congratulations if you have 'your hater'. First make sure your hater is not just genuinely curious. For the real haters, give your team proper training. Remember:

1. Do not delete - respond

2. Be kind and graceful

3. Each comment, even the negative ones, mean more visibility

4. Redirect conversation from social media (providing email, phone contact)

5. Block those who are really rude

6. Consider including comms / liaison with your PR team

Challenge 9: English is a second language of our Ambassadors

You may lead an international team of Ambassadors or you strive to have a global LinkedIn presence in various countries worldwide. We will go into this in detail in Chapter 5, but in this chapter, we want to focus on posting when English is not the first language of your Ambassadors. Getting this right is crucial if you want to tackle global presence.

We have found that even though an Ambassador speaks and writes excellent English, they may have the feeling that their English is not good enough to attract talent, clients and, especially, the media. This can paralyse their content creation and requires time and support. Many Ambassadors will never admit they have this fear of being judged.

For us it was a powerful shift when we realised how valuable our knowledge of various languages, countries and cultures was. Now we know that it is one of the major reasons why our clients decide to work with us.

Solution

Explain this reframe to your Ambassadors:

- Only 3% of conversations in English at this moment worldwide happen between two native speakers. Ninety-seven per cent involve a non-native speaker.[22]

- People do not listen to you despite your accent. The *right people* listen to you *because they like* your accent.

- If you use your second language, you tend to use more simple vocabulary even if you are advanced in that language. This makes topics like tech easy to understand, even for native speakers.

- You will be judged anyway, as a partner, parent, colleague or boss, even speaking your first language. Just dance with the fear. It is well worth it.

Building confidence and supporting your teammates is a step you can't afford to miss. Deal with it as soon as possible, and your team will be ready to rule your niche worldwide.

---

22 M Pascal, 'Learning a language? Speak it like you're playing a video game', TEDx Penang Road (11 May 2017), www.youtube.com/watch?v=Ge7c7otG2mk, accessed 6 May 2023

Challenge 10: What if someone head-hunts our Ambassadors?

Your colleagues are already receiving job offers on LinkedIn. With 15 years of head-hunting experience, we assure you that a satisfied colleague will not leave. So, give them a reason to stay, a great employee experience, because job offers are everywhere, whether on LinkedIn or during lunch with their friend.

Solution

Choose your Ambassadors wisely and their loyalty and the loyalty of other colleagues will increase. Teach them that being an Ambassador is an honour. Head-hunters are looking for dissatisfied people. Ambassadors sharing their employee experience remind themselves and their colleagues what they love about working for your company and why they want to stay.

Nervous system response and its impact on content creation

We have found a surprising reason why people are not showing up on LinkedIn as they want to. Sometimes they still find it challenging, despite their willingness, focus and effort. The dysregulated nervous system often plays a significant role in the struggle to post regularly or authentically. According to Dr M Ruscio,

'A dysregulated nervous system occurs when there is an imbalance between the sympathetic and parasympathetic branches of the autonomic nervous system.'[23] This may sound too medical but stick with us and it will all make sense in the end.

Our nervous system, which includes the brain and spinal cord, is like the command centre of our bodies. It controls things from our thoughts and emotions to vital processes like breathing, heart rate, movement and body temperature.[24] One crucial part of this system is the vagus nerve. It carries information from the brain's surface to tissues and organs elsewhere in the body. One of its key roles is to help keep our nervous system in balance.[25]

Now, you might wonder what this has to do with being visible online. In his book *Why Zebras Don't Get Ulcers: The Acclaimed Guide to Stress, Stress-Related Diseases, and Coping*, Dr Robert Sapolsky, a renowned neuroscientist and professor at Stanford University, explains how stress activates our nervous system.[26]

---

23 M Ruscio, 'A Dysregulated Nervous System: The Overlooked Cause of Emotional and Physical Burnout', Dr Ruscio (10 February 2023), https://drruscio.com/dysregulated-nervous-system, accessed 10 June 2023

24 T Newman, 'All About the Central Nervous System', *Medical News Today* (12 December 2022), www.medicalnewstoday.com/articles/307076, accessed 10 June 2023

25 T Seymour, 'Everything you need to know about the vagus nerve', *Medical News Today* (26 June 2023), www.medicalnewstoday.com/articles/318128#What-is-the-vagus-nerve, accessed 25 June 2023

26 RM Sapolsky, *Why Zebras Don't Get Ulcers: The Acclaimed Guide to Stress, Stress-Related Diseases, and Coping*, Third Edition (Henry Holt and Co, 2004)

It is fascinating how our own bodies quickly start to feel self-doubt, hesitation and inadequacy when we:

- See other people being harshly judged or criticised online or offline for their opinions

- Are stressed and overworked

- Have faced ridicule or backlash for expressing ourselves in the past

Stress may trigger responses, making us feel overwhelmed, lethargic, or ineffective – but that doesn't mean we are incapable. It's simply a biological response to external factors. We have connected the four common types of stress responses with content creation:

1. **Flight:** You may constantly re-write posts or spend hours, even days, contemplating them. You may question whether you should even engage on LinkedIn at all.

2. **Freeze:** Procrastination becomes your companion as you repeatedly delay activities and posts. You may convince yourself that engaging on LinkedIn is not worth it or won't work for your business. There may be a lingering sense of shame for not taking the leap, and you may resist exploring new opportunities.

3. **Fight:** The fight response emerges when you firmly believe only your perspective is correct. You may dismiss the ideas of others, convinced

that they won't work. Explosive or strongly dismissive reactions to other people's suggestions may become apparent.

4. **Fawn:** If you find yourself fawning, you create surface-level and general content, not expressing opinions to avoid conflict and please others.

There are hundreds of activities you can choose to add to your daily routine to cultivate a sense of calm, focus and peace. For the purpose of this Project, consider implementing the following techniques regularly to restore a sense of calm and focus. We use them to regulate our nervous systems and prepare more powerful content with the feeling of ease. These are the top five that work for us:

1. Take a walk outdoors, away from distractions and stimuli. Immerse yourself in nature's calming environment and allow your nervous system to find its balance.

2. Ground yourself by walking barefoot or working with clay and soil, feeling the textures beneath your feet or hands.

3. Shake your body vigorously, releasing tension and promoting the release of excess emotions stored in the body.

4. Press your feet into the ground or lean against a sturdy object like a chair. This physical contact helps anchor your body, bringing a sense of stability.

5. Any form of expressive or mindful movement like dance, yoga or tai chi which allows you to release tension and restore balance in your nervous system. We encourage you to try something new, eg, The Class by Taryn Toomey is an unconventional workout that brings your nervous system regulation to a new level.[27]

Understanding the nervous system responses is crucial because it significantly impacts content creation and life in general. Of course, the central nervous system can be severely dysregulated, but we are intentionally not talking about deep trauma response here. This needs to be addressed with medical professionals. Our intention is to bring to your awareness how daily life situations can trigger the nervous system negatively, but these five techniques can help you to keep the Project on track.

Does it always mean that our dysregulated nervous system is acting up when we do not feel like doing something? Of course not. We all have days when we do not feel like posting. We also like to disconnect and rest. What helps during these times is to have evergreen content ready to be posted anytime.

---

27 K Eldor, 'How Fitness Phenomenon The Class by Taryn Toomey Went From Boutique Studio to Global Stage', *Forbes* (6 May 2020), www.forbes.com/sites/karineldor/2020/05/06/how-online-streaming-helped-workout-phenomenon-the-class-by-taryn-toomey-go-from-boutique-studio-to-global-stage/?sh=30d4a5039efc, accessed 25 June 2023

Evergreen content

Consistent content creation is one of the biggest challenges your Ambassadors will face. Some people wait for inspiration to strike and find it doesn't come. Because of this, it's important to develop a routine that allows you to create content regularly, whether you feel inspired or not.

You might think that when you create posts in advance, they will be irrelevant in a few days or weeks, but there is a way to create evergreen content in bulk months in advance. How can you create evergreen content that stands the test of time? For example, a post about the new iPhone is not evergreen; a post about why people need to implement new information within 48 hours after training is evergreen for years to come.

Choose timeless topics. Instead of writing about the latest events, focus on fundamental principles that your readers will find helpful no matter what's happening in the world. Create 'How to' guides providing practical tips and advice that your followers can apply in their daily work and personal lives.

Use stories. They make your content more engaging and memorable. Use anecdotes, examples, and case studies relevant to fundamental principles, not the latest trends. Write about your values and company culture, which will probably not change in months to come. Answer the FAQs that people ask you all the time about your industry, position or company, record a relevant tutorial or prepare an infographic. Here are some examples of what evergreen content can look like:

- Your questions answered: FAQs about customer experience in retail

- The banker's ultimate guide to building a solid company culture

- The top three benefits of cloud accounting for B2B businesses

- Surprising hacks to optimise your headlines for more engagement

- Seven mistakes you're making on LinkedIn that will ruin your employer brand

Creating evergreen content is a discipline that takes time and effort, but it's worth it. We have clients who craft their content months in advance. They can create, on average, 10–20 high-quality pieces of evergreen content in a day. That accounts for 6 months of evergreen content you can mix with time-sensitive and trendy topics and events. This way, your Ambassadors will not stop because they lack new inspiration, ideas or motivation. They will always have a few pieces of content to pull from the drawer when they do not feel like creating.

When you do not teach your Ambassadors how to tap into the power of evergreen, there will be times when they tell you they do not want to post just for the sake of posting something and that they can't think of anything to write. Weeks go by, and it is hard for them to start creating again. Try to think ahead and help them to understand how relieved they will be when a few posts are ready to be used, not time-sensitive and trendy for months to come.

Content creation is a habit, not a talent. Your Ambassadors must show up at least once a week, whether they feel inspired or not. Developing a consistent content creation routine is vital and will help them when their motivation inevitably slumps.

As Elizabeth Gilbert, an author who has sold millions of books worldwide, says in her book *Big Magic: Creative Living Beyond Fear*, perfectionism, originality and passion are overrated. Instead, we should strive to be authentic doers who follow our curiosity.[28]

---

28 E Gilbert, *Big Magic: Creative Living Beyond Fear* (Riverhead Books, 2016)

Summary

In this chapter, we have covered the following:

- What content creation is
- How to give attention to things that matter
- Top ten biggest challenges when it comes to content creation
- Solutions for these challenges
- Creating evergreen content

FOUR
Practical Content Creation

Now you know your goals, how to get colleagues on board, and how to structure your Ambassador Team. We've also covered the top ten challenges when it comes to team content creation and the solutions you can apply. In this chapter, we will dive deeper into practical tips for team content creation that wins hearts, talent and clients on a bigger scale.

Define the Lead

You are not here to please everyone, and there is zero chance you will. One of the main goals of your content is to deselect those who do not resonate with your personality and company values. This way, you get a loyal tribe of followers who will be glad to consume your content regularly.

If your budget is not unlimited and you do not want to wait years for results, focus on being different. Being different attracts exactly who you want to attract – your Lead – whether that is a potential client, business partner, colleague or investor. It may even be a journalist who might give PR opportunities such as participating in podcasts for free. Your Lead is the key person your company either wants to work with, have work for them or collaborate with.

Be sure you know who you are talking to. Focus on a specific group, and tailor the message to their pains, preferences and interests. Your communication will instantly become more effective and impactful.

Content creation might seem complex if you have various product ranges, services and departments hiring or active across various industries. It also changes with time. Start simple – aim for a maximum of two types of Leads for each Ambassador. You can evaluate it later when you are used to tailoring your communication to a particular persona.

Your Leads might not even be on social media. If not, start thinking about who knows these people and whether you can refer your work directly to them. For example, you may be trying to find workers for your factory right now. If that's the case, revisit your personal and company goal in Chapter 1 and now think about your Leads:

- What newspapers do they read? What channels do they watch on TV? Your Ambassador can do some investigative work to find a contact on LinkedIn who might be a journalist from that newspaper or TV station. That is your Lead and your Ambassador can then suggest collaborations such as writing articles that will resonate with your ideal candidates who are also their audience.

- Are any similar companies in the region downsizing? The HR Manager becomes your Lead. You can offer them cooperation on an outplacement project.

- Who is connected to the person you want to connect with? Are their family members on LinkedIn? Sometimes your Lead is not readily obvious. It could be your potential colleague´s teacher or wife.

There are many ways to get to anyone you need to if you brainstorm ideas long enough.

✏ ACTION STEP

Choose the Lead that you want to attract the most. Think about your Lead's:

- Job position
- Biggest work challenge

- Primary work goal
- Interests and dreams

Write down your thoughts. Try to define your ideal Lead in five words.

Create content that converts

You've probably seen the kind of viral post with a cute kitty or a useless poll asking if you prefer coffee or coke at work. It gets thousands of likes and hundreds of comments, and you cannot believe it. Who engages with this type of post on a professional platform? Well, you must realise that many LinkedIn users do not have other social media, or do not use it actively. The only place where they are exposed to kitties is LinkedIn. The critical question is, do these people who claim to have millions of views get any business opportunities through this kind of content?

We believe that three likes from potential clients are way better than three hundred from random people who do not know what you do. Everyone is different, and so is content type and creation. Constantly revisit the goals you have set in Chapter 1 to make sure your content is leading you towards them.

What can you expect from posting regularly and implementing a content strategy? Let us tell you about our client, the SME tech company formerly known only among the local tech community. After completing several pieces of training, their LinkedIn star was born. The number of their Company Page followers increased by more than 500% in a year. People outside the tech community started to recognise them, and event attendees even seek them out to discuss, particular LinkedIn posts. Tomáš Lodňan is ranked among the best CEO LinkedIn profiles in the region. And GoodRequest is regularly ranked among the largest tech companies on LinkedIn in their region. What makes GoodRequest so special? Their culture, attitude, energy and drive towards their goal.

The golden rule of balanced content

How do you create content that is professional, but feels personal? It is easier to start with content that is purely business. Add a little spark by using your opinions so they are not purely announcements. Once you and your team get more experienced, you can create more personal posts. Even personal posts can be tied to your work or business. For example, our client, Veronika, who talked about taking a walk and ended up with a new client. Our client's Ambassador in the tech industry posted his wedding photo and, magically, all the big fish in his industry started sending him invites to connect.

It does not have to be the marketing department that is solely responsible for content. Our client, the Sales Director for DACH at an IT company called Stengl, crafted a single LinkedIn post with a strategically selected image and impactful wording. The outcome? He found a new client from Germany which led to a collaboration where Stengl now supplies a sixteen-member IT team and covers the entire test management. Our client FLORIL, an exclusive patisserie, successfully attracts corporate clients and large retailers with the CEO's content and became the market leader through creating meaningful relationships.

LinkedIn algorithm

If you need more change in your life, start studying the LinkedIn algorithm. It changes rapidly. You finally figure it out, and it changes in a couple of days. That is why you should not focus on the newest information according to the LinkedIn algorithm. Instead, focus on the logic behind it. That way, you will never be stuck on which format to use, and how.

The easy rule of thumb is: 'Follow the money'. Think as a LinkedIn founder. Where do you earn money? From ads and paid services. Keep your audience entertained on the platform and you cannot lose. The more your followers stay, the more LinkedIn makes. That pleases the algorithm, so it gives you more opportunities to do it again and again by exposing the content of your Ambassadors and Company Page to more viewers.

Do not move conversations from LinkedIn. This is a common mistake. People start their conversations on LinkedIn and instantly ask for an email address. You will lose many opportunities. LinkedIn is based on AI. It needs to have data to learn from. If LinkedIn can see that you have deeper conversations with a particular person, it will show you similar profiles and more relevant content. Your content also becomes more visible to the person you have a conversation with.

If a team member is number and data-oriented and loves to dig into algorithms, tools and spreadsheets then let them go through your Company Page analytics every month. The tool is very useful for data lovers.

Each country has its specifics. If you follow LinkedIn experts, choose those with their data for the specific region you are interested in. When we compare the US and Europe, we see huge differences, even in Europe on national levels. Follow experts who have global experience.

When it comes to the LinkedIn algorithm, always test everything you read about for yourselves and see what works.

Content types and formats

When you want your Team to create content, they will have various options. They will ask which type of content has the highest engagement rate. As the LinkedIn algorithm changes, its favourite content types vary.

If your team is just starting, let them create in a way that feels natural to them. If they love visual content, they may use their own pictures. If they love to write, they can create longer text posts, articles and newsletters. If they feel confident creating videos, let them do it. If they love to improvise, let them create LinkedIn lives.

LinkedIn also thinks of those who are more introverted. Sometimes, they launch new formats, which always aim to encourage content creators – for example, polls, templates, celebrating occasions and kudos. If you click on the three dots in the right-hand section of a post on LinkedIn, you can explore what is available at the time. These are simple ways to engage Cheerleaders in creating content, too.

You and your team can express your creativity as you like. You can apply your brand guidelines, but do not force your Ambassadors to use only branded content. If they use their own visuals, they will be more recognisable. Their face helps deliver their content to a bigger audience. Using it to bring attention to various ideas, topics and trends is a smart move, not a way to show off. This will create a special bond between your team and their followers. And, of course, trust is the key to every successful relationship.

People want to connect with other people much more than brands. So, if your Ambassadors are brave enough, use video to connect with your ideal Leads in an authentic way. The easiest way to help them do this is to interview the Ambassador or a combination of the Ambassador and another expert. A 1-minute video is perfect. That means that with one interview, they can create evergreen content that they can use any time they cannot find their muse.

From our experience, letting your Ambassadors create content without control gets the most out of their creativity. They can surprise their followers with different formats, visuals and video styles. Each Ambassador has to find an authentic style that suits their ideal Leads.

TOP TIP

Visibility is important. Fortunately, you do not have to post every single day on LinkedIn. What is more important is the value your team brings. So, start posting once a week and then show your love to your audience and Leads by supporting their content with comments and likes. You can even recommend them to others by tagging them in relevant posts.

The 5-ingredient method for content creation

Do not rely on inspiration to appear magically every week. That's why we've got your back if you want to create content systematically with a clear strategy.

We have developed a 5-ingredient method for content creation that will prevent you from staring at a blank page.

Creating content in bulk, in advance, has a disadvantage because you are not writing about something you are experiencing in the moment. The advantage of using evergreen posts is that this gives you the freedom to use them at any time. Think of topics that involve your values, strengths, niche trends, company culture, etc.

Let's talk about the numbers first. Each Ambassador and Company Page should create two posts per week, ideally. Therefore, for one month, you will need eight posts for each of the Ambassadors' personal profiles and eight posts for the Company Page. It may seem a lot, but with the 5-ingredient method, you will manage to do it with ease. Go to the Resources section, download our implementation playsheets and start this exciting content creation journey with us. There are some simple action steps for Ambassadors to answer at the end of each ingredient before moving on to the next one.

Ingredient 1: Time pressure

Nothing helps you create faster than time pressure. Otherwise, your team will procrastinate for weeks. Have dedicated time for content creation. You have these three options:

1. Get your Ambassadors together once a month for 90 minutes. Brainstorm for the first 30 minutes and then sit and write for rest of your meeting. Afterwards, the Ambassadors need to schedule a 1-hour session in their own diaries to finish their posts. These group coworking sessions bring an incredible feeling of community and support.

2. Each Ambassador has a LinkedIn date in their diary for 2 hours once a month. They need to treat it as a regular meeting that is non-negotiable. They are on a mission to create at least eight posts ready to go in those 2 hours.

3. Get a professional sparring partner. The hardest thing is to sit and start. Professional LinkedIn experts and copywriters have a helicopter view and a specific method to do it fast. They can help you find your voice and create content effectively.

✏ ACTION STEP

Choose how to apply time pressure to your project.

Ingredient 2: Your life in images

With this ingredient, you and your team will get inspiration from your own phone gallery. You do not have to use the actual picture. This step will give you the inspiration to create. Your phone galleries may seem full of your favourite places, pets, food or kids.

The secret *sauce* ingredient is the feeling and story that comes with the picture. The one you took on your first day at work or the one baking a new cake for the first time. The feelings might be similar, and they will spark inspiration to tell a story: a professional or a personal one. Open your heart and keep your LinkedIn goal in your mind, then look at your life in images and use them as inspiration.

✎ AMBASSADOR'S ACTION STEP

Choose at least five pictures as inspiration.

Build a story around your picture and create your post in your scheduled creative time.

Ingredient 3: A great question is the best answer

Let your Ambassadors imagine they are guests in their favourite podcast. The host asks them a question, and they just answer without a long introduction. Have a special section in your content creation system for powerful questions. Nothing else will boost your creativity like this. You can start with these questions:

- If you could go back and give your 20-year-old-self one piece of advice, what would it be?

- What's the best compliment you've ever received?

- Who are your three most influential mentors, and how have they impacted you?

✎ **AMBASSADOR'S ACTION STEP**

Write down your three favourite questions.

Ingredient 4: Recycle your posts

Your Ambassadors have some golden nuggets in their previous posts on their personal profiles. During their scheduled creative time, ask each Ambassador to go through their LinkedIn activities. Here are some examples of what they can do to repurpose old content:

- Is there a post that did not resonate with your audience that much? Re-write it and share it again. Change the format or picture.

- Did you receive relevant answers from a poll you created? Screenshot results, create interesting graphics and share the results.

- Did you share a story that continues? Share the next episode.

- Did you have a viral post with several impressions or likes that surprised you? Create a post about it.

✏ **AMBASSADOR'S ACTION STEP**

Choose three posts to repurpose.

Ingredient 5: Do not reinvent the wheel

Your Company Page admins work very hard to create consistently high-quality content that catches followers' attention. The Ambassadors can help them to spread the word across your LinkedIn network. Start with a comment. This will help both your personal brands and the Company Page, too.

Reuse company posts to create more buzz around the topic. Ten people can talk about the same thing and it will be different every time.

TOP TIP

When repurposing content, ensure your reader will not notice. The easiest way is to change the visuals. Picture or video is the first thing your audience will see. Even if you use the same picture with entirely new text, it will still look like an old post. Change the picture, and you can recapture attention.

Every Ambassador has a different point of view, different feelings and experiences. When reusing a post, think about the topic from your perspective. Even if you are paraphrasing, it is a unique post.

✎ AMBASSADOR'S ACTION STEPS

- Show love for company content with a comment on your Company Page.
- Re-write a company post, use a different visual and post it.

Content hubs – the secret to staying organised

Let's face it – keeping track of all the ideas, drafts, and published content can be a nightmare for one person, let alone when you have a team creating regularly. That's where content hubs come in: they're like the trusty sidekick that helps you stay organised, focused and on top of your content game.

Content hubs are a must-have if you're looking to leverage employee advocacy on LinkedIn. Why? Because they make it easy for your colleagues to create, manage, and distribute content joyfully. Plus, they're a great way to showcase your expertise, build your thought leadership and engage with your audience. Win-win, right?

Company content hub

The company content hub is a place where your Ambassadors and Cheerleaders go for inspiration, visuals, guidelines and training to create their own content. This way they will not call you every time they need a photo or information. Your company content hub serves for all colleagues who want to participate in your LinkedIn adventure. Each Ambassador can also create their own personal content hub.

First let's look at three ways to create a company content hub that works.

1. Decide on a structure for your content hub

Think of your content hub as a filing cabinet. You want to have different folders for different types of content. Having a structure in place will make it easier for your Ambassadors and Cheerleaders to find what they need when they need it. You will find out what works for you in the process. Start with a simple structure like:

- Approved visual content (pictures, videos, presentations, infographics and data)

- Texts they can use as inspiration

- LinkedIn toolkits, video training, templates and checklists

- LinkedIn cover photos to choose from

2. Choose a tool or software for your content hub

There are plenty of tools out there that can help you manage your content hub. You can use any project management software for a simple solution. Use a simple four-folder structure listed in Point 1. You can also use LinkedIn's Company Pages features to:

- Pre-write content in the My Company section – use only bullet points and the Ambassadors and Cheerleaders can make it their own so it becomes an original post with their own wording

- See the Trending Content feature and curate it for your audience

- Automatically show your employees' content on your Company Page when they use your approved hashtags and are connected with your Company Pages as an employee

Consider a specialised Ambassador Project software if you have thousands of Cheerleaders in your company. The features you might find helpful are:

- Content library with pre-approved content and visuals

- Social media scheduling

- Detailed analytics and reporting

- Gamification and incentives

We purposefully do not mention specific software solutions as IT and AI move quickly, but you are welcome to get in touch for recommendations when you read this book. Just make sure you choose a tool that's easy to use, has the features you need, and that your colleagues will use.

You already know that just giving your colleagues new software will not be the solution; you must go through all the steps in this book to make sure your Employee Ambassadors know why, how and what to do.

Our client, Lidl, one of the leading retailers in Europe, understood each colleague's LinkedIn presence directly impacted their employer brand value. They decided to take their colleagues' interest in this social network to the next level.

The Project followed a clear LinkedIn education plan ranging from bare LinkedIn essentials webinars through to content creation sessions and detailed content workshops.

The team went from saying 'I don't know what to write' or 'No one will be interested in this' to feeling comfortable creating content. All it took was a plan, a consistent approach and a few tips along the way.

Writing one post is not enough however, so the Ambassador Project was introduced to ensure continuity. The Project is voluntary and Lidl's employer branding department continuously works with the

Ambassadors to guide them. They even introduced motivational competitions to support and build a positive posting habit.

Lidl continue to be amazed at how successful the content the employees create is. Significant benefits are also evident when recruiting. Now, the candidates give feedback that they follow the company and the Ambassadors on LinkedIn, and that's why they applied for the role.

3. Maintain and update your content hub regularly

Regularly review, update and optimise your content to keep it fresh, relevant and engaging. That might involve reviewing and updating old content, analysing metrics to see what's working, and collaborating with others to keep your content hub up-to-date.

Creating a content hub may sound like hard work, but trust us – it's worth it. By having a centralised location for all your content, your colleagues will always know where to go when they want to:

- Update their profiles
- Create high-quality content
- Add value to their followers
- Get inspired and not wait for motivation
- Uplevel their LinkedIn game with training and support

Personal content hub

Creating great content takes time, effort and a bit of magic. It also needs a system. To make sure you're consistently producing high-quality content, develop a workflow that works for you.

Each Ambassador should have a content hub, preferably synchronised over various devices you use. Some catch their ideas as voice messages, some print-screen interesting articles or posts, and some have a beautiful notebook at hand. All of that is OK as long it works for you. For your mobile phone and PC, you can use the following folders:

- An 'Ideas' folder for all visuals, print-screens and photos of inspiration and voice messages.

- A 'Drafts' folder for storing all posts ready to go on LinkedIn if you create them in advance.

- A 'Published content' folder to store content that has already been published. This is great for repurposing, because LinkedIn only keeps your content for a limited period of time.

Find a system that includes brainstorming ideas, researching, outlining, writing, editing and proofreading your content. Yes, that means even you, creative souls, that roll your eyes reading this!

Artificial Intelligence for content creation

It's no surprise that AI has become a significant topic of business conversations in recent years. With its potential to transform how businesses communicate, operate and even innovate, AI can have tremendous implications for success or failure. When it comes to content creation, AI's ability to enable hyper-personalisation of content is a significant breakthrough. By studying user data, AI can generate personalised content aligned with individual user needs. As with any new technology, there are both sceptics and early adopters when it comes to adopting AI within organisations and which side you land on will define your path forwards.

Whatever your opinion on the capabilities of AI, as a Project Hero, you might need to navigate this topic with your team. There are two camps of people you will probably have in your Project team and this is how they can use AI to make the content process faster and more enjoyable:

The sceptic

The sceptic usually feels that content by AI is nowhere near as good as human creation but also fears that AI will take away the need for content created by humans. The sceptic will need time to move beyond the fear and recognise what AI can offer for faster content creation. Do not push any Ambassador to use AI, even if you think it is a great idea.

The best way to convince a sceptic to try AI tools is to show them that AI can be found in nearly any sector – from autonomous cars to increasingly sophisticated home assistants that have become integral parts of daily life. Your Ambassador probably uses it daily without even noticing (eg, tools like Spotify, Canva, Grammarly, Zoom, Google or any social media platform). AI is here to stay. We predict that AI's role in producing creative content will be enormous in the future, but this presents both an opportunity and a threat.

AI is creating unique opportunities for Ambassadors to generate compelling content faster, more accurately and more efficiently than ever before. If they're ready to get on board, technology can move their industry forwards and help leaders reach their goals more quickly. The risks are also significant though. They include inaccuracies of information, intellectual property infringement, dependency on technology, lack of creativity, increasing noise, loss of control over the content and even reputational risks. You need people on your team who can look into the future and recognise what these risks are. These are your sceptics.

If some of your team members are sceptics, but willing to try, then support them by introducing tools that make their lives easier, for example, translating text at lightning speed, using a grammar check or brainstorming ideas with AI tools.

The early adopter

This person finds AI fascinating. They can already see how you can replace 90% of your content creation and create on scale. All the tasks that used to need a professional team can be done with a few clicks on your phone. The question for the early adopter is how to ensure their content does not look automated. It must feel authentic and personal, or it will get lost in the ocean of AI-created content. You can find tutorials like 'How to create 30 pieces of content from scratch in 10 minutes, using only AI' and there are many people applying this to their social media. As it becomes much easier to fake expertise, there will be so much more noise in social media. If you want your content to stand out, you will need to use a more human touch. AI for content creation is not only writing the post, but also:

- Brainstorming content ideas

- Research

- Grammar checks and translation

- Data collection and analysis

- Content personalisation

- Optimising keywords for SEO

- Assisting with the writing process according to your goals

- Making content more accessible for people with disabilities

- Generating captions
- Auto-generation of infographics
- Repurposing content into various formats
- Creating and editing images, music and videos from texts

AI is advancing at a blinding pace. If you adapt and learn, you can use intelligent automation without worrying about losing control of your creative out-puts. Early adopters already know that content can be created ten times faster with the current technology. Using AI technologies enables them to focus on the parts of content creation they find most interesting. It is like having a great executive assistant on hand, who may astound you with the results. However, you need to know how to command the task.

Summary

In this chapter, we have covered the following:

- Why and how to define your Lead
- How to achieve content that converts
- Types of content for every type of creator
- The 5-ingredient Method of content creation
- AI content creation for sceptics and early adopters

FIVE

Unique Structure For Your LinkedIn Presence

For years, companies talked to us about building their Company Pages without using personal profiles. Some of them reused the content from their website or blogs and some used corporate content from their headquarters. Often, it resulted in very low engagement. They wanted to change that, but to increase engagement they needed to build a unique structure for their LinkedIn presence that included both personal profiles and Company Pages.

Years went by, and now companies increasingly understand that people want to connect with, and buy from, people. You already know the easiest way is to use company Ambassadors. But how do you combine these two different worlds of personal profiles and Company Pages? Let's look at them as two ingredients you want to mix in a particular way and order.

Structures for the best results

Every company has unique challenges, goals and budgets. It influences how the structure for their LinkedIn presence looks and what activities you need to do in a particular order. LinkedIn gives you the possibilities to create a structure that works for your company.

In this chapter we will share the three structures that we see the most so that you can be inspired and see what works for you. All structures include a Company Page. If you are reading this book, you have big goals. Big goals need the support of a Company Page.

Structure # 1: One Global LinkedIn Company Page

This structure is straightforward and easy to manage, making it attractive for small- to medium-sized companies. However, its simplicity comes with a downside. A single global page may lack the regional specificity needed to engage different markets effectively. As you scale your operations, localising your content can become crucial for audience engagement and relevance.

This is where most international companies start. They create one Global LinkedIn Company Page and offer corporate content to regions. It is a great start. Your colleagues can connect their profiles to your Company Page, support the content and show the world you dominate a particular niche worldwide. Through your Global LinkedIn Company Page, you can have more control over the content that is posted. However, smaller regions often feel they are invisible. So much content is generated worldwide that their local posts, even those targeted to a particular region, get lost. They often feel corporate topics do not apply to a particular location, and the local admin teams do not have access and/or motivation to invite followers to the global page.

Some local employees create a local page and become admins. They do not ask for permission, but after gaining a few thousand followers, they ask for forgiveness. We have yet to see a company that decides to delete a local page with a decent following! However, we recommend you follow the rules. Prepare a business case to demonstrate that a local page is crucial for your LinkedIn growth, create a B2B community of supporters and increase your Ambassadors' motivation. If you are not allowed to create your local Company Page, use Ambassadors' personal profiles to localise what you need.

This structure works perfectly even if you strongly desire to create product LinkedIn sub-pages. If you do not work for a large corporation or suspect that no one in the company will be able to manage it all, keep it simple at the beginning, with one Global LinkedIn Company Page. Divide your product or service portfolio using Ambassadors' personal profiles first. As time passes, you may need to create more Company Pages.

Personal profiles drive the Ambassador Project. They are perfect not only for small companies or solopreneurs, but even for multinational corporations. It is because people love human-to-human marketing and because it gives you the freedom to create on a different level.

Each Ambassador has a unique set of goals, audience, KPIs, language skills, know-how and voice. Just imagine how much your team can do with the combination of global support and local insights and know-how. When you are helping your Ambassadors to find their voice, do not forget that they should talk about your company at least 50% of the time. An Ambassador is not a real Ambassador when they do not talk about your vision, culture, values and successes.

It is very common for global companies to have only one LinkedIn Page. Our client, global consultancy EY, localised their content and decided to build their local presence through the personal profiles of key leaders and senior staff. We organised an inspirational presentation for up to 100 of their employees. It included vital technical information, the reasons for their decision, and tips on building a personal brand to support the company brand.

Structure # 2: The multi-page structure

There are endless ways for companies to build their B2B presence on LinkedIn. Later in their LinkedIn journey companies start to experiment with and add to Structure # 1 by adding more Company Pages. They create a complicated matrix of different pages over time. Companies usually start to experiment with various Company Pages for each:

- Country

- Product/service range

- Particular product

- Subsidiary

- Daughter company

With such a variety of Company Pages, their LinkedIn presence becomes so complex that they often get lost. They do not know where to post a particular achievement or information, as it usually applies to more than one Company Page. And the biggest challenge? Content creation. Maintaining a regular stream of localised, relevant content across multiple pages is labour-intensive. When followers are spread thinly across various pages, there's also a risk of diluted engagement and potentially missed content. This complexity, however, may be worth it if your company is large enough, and each page serves a distinctive purpose that aligns with your overall strategy.

Some companies have dozens of Company Pages. This becomes complicated and unsustainable. You want to create a structure that is clear and easy to follow. This strategic umbrella is ideally created on a global level. Then all countries feel more empowered and confident to create on their own.

Most companies, even with thousands of employees, do not have a person who manages the LinkedIn strategy solely. It is usually done in various countries, through various departments or teams, and mixed with other social media or marketing activities. But this B2B tool which is responsible for generating 80% of B2B leads worldwide[29] deserves much more attention.

This is where you come into play as the Project Hero. It does not matter if you create a small local or a huge global Ambassador Team. With a clear strategy, everything becomes easier. We have witnessed local Ambassador Projects become global after they were tested in small areas. Make the life of your colleagues easier, and you are on the right path.

Structure # 3: The individual structure

The 'individual' structure is elusive because it's unique to each company and dependent on numerous

---

29 'The case for B2B marketing on LinkedIn', LinkedIn Ads Blog (16 November 2016), www.linkedin.com/business/marketing/blog/ linkedin-ads/get-proof-the-case-for-b2b-marketing-on-linkedin-infographic, accessed 6 November 2023

factors. These include your company's goals, the size of your Ambassador Team, the company guidelines, and even the number of Ambassadors advocating for your company on LinkedIn.

The individual structure should strike a balance between a single global page and multiple, distinct pages. For instance, if your company operates globally but has a robust presence in certain regions, having regional pages alongside the global one could be beneficial. This structure provides localised content while maintaining a unified brand image.

Your company's policies also play a role. For example, if your company guidelines allow for greater regional autonomy, localised pages could be an excellent way to capitalise on local knowledge and engagement. If, however, your company prefers a consistent, global image then a single global page might serve you better.

The size of your team also plays a critical role in determining your optimal structure. For example, some companies have whole social media teams (content creation, admins, paid ads, etc). A larger team might handle multiple pages efficiently, while smaller teams might struggle with the same task. Keep in mind that resources spent on managing multiple pages might be better invested in training staff or creating higher-quality content for fewer pages.

The optimal structure may seem like a complex puzzle, but it essentially boils down to aligning your LinkedIn

THE MAGIC OF EMPLOYEE INFLUENCE

presence with your strategic goals, company guide-lines, team resources and Ambassador strength. And remember, the optimal structure for your company today may change in the future as these variables evolve. Staying flexible and ready to adapt is key to maintaining a successful and relevant LinkedIn presence.

To identify the ideal structure, we have a detailed discussion with the Project Guardian and the Project Hero – on the global and local level. That way we meet the goals, but make it as simple as possible.

Personal profile vs Company Page (reaching vs anchoring)

Having discussed the three main structures, let's dive deeper into the differences between personal profiles and Company Pages, the main roles of each, and how they can benefit your company.

Big goals require both personal profiles and Company Pages. Each has a different role and different pros and cons. Combining the two brings the most powerful results for your Ambassador Project.

Personal profile

Richard Branson has 20m followers on LinkedIn, yet the company he founded – Virgin Atlantic, has only

300,000 followers. Can you see the difference? This is what great personal branding does.

Even for companies that are widely known, it is impossible to have a higher reach than their employees combined. If you have a formal Ambassador Project, your employees combined have more than ten times higher reach of the whole company because the most memorable content typically involves a particular person's story.

Personal profiles create a platform where Ambassadors learn, network and connect with like-minded individuals, and existing and potential colleagues and clients. They share their expertise while growing the company brand. They can join and engage in industry-specific conversations and groups to increase visibility and become thought leaders for a particular topic. Employee advocacy thrives on vibrant personal profiles, creative content and engaging conversations.

In the case of small companies, there is a significant opportunity to focus primarily on personal profiles as a marketing strategy. Our client, the owner of ENTERIS, a leading company in public procurement, took this approach and experienced the remarkable impact of LinkedIn. Prior to leveraging LinkedIn, their marketing efforts included various channels such as TV, newspapers, Instagram, Facebook and Google Ads. However, after the owner began building her brand on LinkedIn, it became their primary and most effective marketing tool alongside Google Ads.

Now, let's address a question that often arises: if a CEO's personal profile is polished and a PR manager occasionally prepares LinkedIn posts, does it make the CEO an Ambassador? From LinkedIn's audience perspective, the CEO will, indeed, be visible as an Ambassador of the company. However, from the viewpoint of the Ambassador Project, the answer is no. To be recognised as an Employee Ambassador, individuals need to actively engage in training, consistently create content, interact with and support other Ambassadors, as well as contribute with ideas for the Company Page. Although they may not officially have a role as Employee Ambassadors, it is still valuable to include the CEO's personal profile within the overall structure though. CEOs are often Project Guardians so they also share unique experiences and insights on the platform in that role.

Company Page

A Company page is so much more than just a place for press releases. It is an umbrella that brings the team together and builds credibility. In addition, having a Company Page gives access to features not available elsewhere – targeted ads, job postings, multi-admin support – enabling potential clients or colleagues to dive straight into your content without any need for searching around. It is like a library, full of exciting information and fresh opinions and ideas from your colleagues and clients.

They also provide detailed statistics about your followers, content performance and audience engagement. The Company Page is a one-stop place for your Cheerleaders to support your content in 5 minutes a week.

It's common for Company Pages to experience slower follower growth compared to personal profiles. However, with the right strategy and a consistent approach, the growth can still be quite rapid. Let's take the example of Swiss Life Select SVK, a leading financial company that managed to achieve remarkable results in less than a year. They were able to grow their follower base by over 300% during this period.

The key to their success was their dedication to consistently providing valuable content. They actively invited individuals from both the offline and online worlds to connect with their page. Additionally, they involved their management team, which further supported their efforts. Their focus extended beyond simply increasing the number of followers; their impression rate also experienced significant growth, surpassing 430%.

This example demonstrates the importance of a comprehensive and sustained approach to growing a LinkedIn Company Page. By consistently delivering valuable content, engaging with a wide audience and involving key stakeholders, it's possible to achieve substantial growth and maximise the reach and impact of your Company Page.

To build and maintain an engaged following requires more effort than personal pages, but LinkedIn invests heavily in making the Company Pages way better. In the last three years, we have seen a major shift in focus, with new features added almost every few weeks. Now, you can enjoy and monetise your Company Pages like never before. LinkedIn is on a mission to create what Amazon did for B2C buyers: an ultimate B2B buying experience directly through the features they are providing. Use your Company Page to anchor your audience and personal profiles to reach further.

Potential risks and how to avoid them

To decide which structure is the best for your Ambassador Project, you should know the risks of each one, too. We've broken down some common challenges in Chapter 3. Below, we have practical examples of the risks that occur when it comes to using personal profiles and Company Pages, and the solutions that will help you avoid costly mistakes.

Personal profile

Situation 1

You have a great and dedicated Ambassador, but he decides to leave the company. Your Ambassador is very visible at this point, and the way he handles leaving the company may impact negatively on the whole project and your company's reputation.

Solution: Ask your Ambassador to write a warm goodbye post or write one yourself that talks about the Ambassador leaving the company in a positive way. Before your Ambassador says goodbye, you should know who will be taking their place. The Ambassador can even introduce the new one and wish them all the best.

Situation 2

Your Ambassador has been in service for a year, but now they are lacking motivation and posting less and less. Some Ambassadors stay active for years while others stop posting after a year or two. What you need to know is this: whatever made them start will not keep them going as Ambassadors.

Solution: You have to revisit their goals and motivation together and find a way to make being an Ambassador attractive again. Maybe their goals have changed. They may need a step up. They could help you train their successor. They could participate in a short-term project, for example, supporting a particular campaign. Or they could become a Project Hero for new territories as you expand your Ambassador Project to new departments or regions.

Situation 3

The Ambassadors start or have their own business they want to promote. If your Cheerleaders want to do other activities, it is not a problem. If your Ambassadors are heavily invested in another projects, you need to act.

Solution: Have an open conversation. If this is against your company rules, change the Ambassadors. If not, revisit the goals from Chapter 1 together. To remain Ambassadors, 80% of the profile and content needs to be about your company, and 20% about other projects or causes the Ambassador cares about. Otherwise, you invest in a people who will not give you the ROI. This point should be included in your social media guidelines.

Company Page

Situation 1

Your Company Page admin leaves and you lose access to your page. It may not seem probable, but we have seen countless companies lose their access to their Company Page. Reasons ranging from, 'We don't know who the admin was historically,' through to, 'There has been a breach on the admin's personal profile,' to, 'He left and does not want to communicate with us.' Getting your access back is extremely difficult, especially if your admin does not want to communicate or you do not know who they are. You might never get it back.

Solution: Always have at least two Company Page admins. We advise having more than five admins in larger companies.

Situation 2

The corporate content does not work and needs to be more authentic. We talked about creating content in Chapters 3 and 4, so you already know that simply reusing visuals from headquarters will rarely attract your Leads.

Solution: Prepare a business case and present it to headquarters. How do your corporate visuals and themes perform in comparison to authentic local content? Go through the statistics together. If you still need to use corporate content, make sure your Ambassadors' comments are relevant to your ideal Leads.

Situation 3

You have only a small number of followers for the impact you want to have.

Solution: An Ambassador Project is your ultimate solution for gaining more followers. The engaged ones. There are many ways to increase your following with Employee Ambassadors, for example:

- Inviting connections from a personal profile

- Redirecting all new personal connections

- Talking about your LinkedIn Company Page in your email marketing

- Using QR codes or buttons in email signatures and during events

- Sending your candidates from interviews directly to follow your company

---

CASE STUDY: VOLTIA

The situation: Voltia, an electromobility company, had a superior product to most competitors globally, but nobody knew about it. An innovative, high-quality product that needed brand awareness to drive sales results. Voltia was active in six countries but had true global potential.

The goal: To increase brand awareness worldwide and drive leads and potential partnerships into the pipeline.

The initial state of LinkedIn: No Company Page, three active users in sales and the total number of followers of all employees combined was below 4,000. The sales manager had 1,800, the sales team another 1,800 combined, and the rest was management and HR. Being unknown made the sales process much more complicated.

The solution: Creating Employee Ambassadors' profiles, training for all employees, KPIs for colleagues and a monthly checklist of LinkedIn activities. The sales and management teams became the Ambassadors, and even the technical team, engineers and all other functions were their targets as Cheerleaders. Later, they introduced lead generation campaigns.

The results: Each team member has 2,000–4,000 active followers from almost sixty countries. The average number of views increased tenfold. They reached global recognition. Their Leads know precisely who they are talking to and how great their product and services are. Currently, they have active clients in nineteen countries: roughly half of them got to know them through LinkedIn first. A portion of these clients admit that they have been convinced by Ambassadors' posts that they are trustworthy and they deliver. Voltia has active business negotiations in another six countries and has received requests from almost all the sixty countries where they have followers.

Global Ambassadors and your LinkedIn presence

The main challenge you will face if you lead an international team of Ambassadors or have a global LinkedIn presence is the language you use on LinkedIn. There are various factors to consider such as:

- What languages do you use for personal profiles?

- How do you use languages in multiple Company Pages?

- Should you have a multilingual Company Page and target specific countries?

- Should you have local pages in the local language?

- Do you start in one country or build Global Ambassadors simultaneously?

According to our own experience and data, LinkedIn users understand English, but very often prefer to consume content in their mother tongue. Your LinkedIn presence depends on your location. Your goals, needs and LinkedIn tools will vary depending on whether you operate in one country, or globally.

Our job is to understand the insights and specifics and prepare the structure for your LinkedIn presence that will work best for you. Some of the structures are more advanced and complicated; some are simpler. To give a proper answer to these questions, you need to know your:

- Company vision

- Current goals

- Ideal Leads

- Sales/candidate funnels

- Existing policies

- Team structure

For now, let's look at the easiest way to build your Global Ambassador team. If you want to start as simply as possible, you have options to create either an Ambassador Team in one country and replicate this in the future to other territories, or a full Global Ambassador Team with one Ambassador per country and then replicate within other departments and territories.

If you are using a software tool where your colleagues are sharing your company content, they are Cheerleaders, not Ambassadors. You cannot have thousands of engaged Ambassadors who take ownership of the Project. What we want you to create is totally different – a Project with colleagues who have an enormous impact and influence on your business growth.

Summary

In this chapter, we have covered:

- Three structures for your LinkedIn presence that you can use

- The pros and cons of Company Pages and personal profiles when it comes to an Ambassador Project

- How to avoid the most common risks

- Introduction to how to handle Global Ambassadors and your global LinkedIn presence

SIX

The 10-hour Launch Plan

A (love) letter to the Project Hero

Dear Project Hero,

You can kick this Project off in just 10 hours, see the first results in 30 days and make it joyful and sustainable for you, the Ambassadors and the whole team. We know it is a bold promise, but we are sure you will be successful. Why? Because you are an action-taker, committed and unstoppable. We will give you the exact steps you need to take. Tried, tested and proven with hundreds of companies like yours.

In this chapter, we will make sure you know a process that makes LinkedIn activities an integral part of the day in the most frictionless way possible. If you give your colleagues the know-how and the process to prepare, prioritise and thrive with your Ambassador Project, you all win. The whole team will see LinkedIn as a professional, fun place and will see what's in it for them. They will thank you for the clear path to success.

We are so proud of the work you have already done. You are the Project Hero in charge. Before you start, there are three things we want from you:

- *Keep your head and heart open to new ideas.*

- *Do not expect it to be easy.*

- *Trust our process.*

Every minute you spend on this Project will give you a massive return on your invested time. Give us 10 hours, and you will see the first results within the next 30 days. Once you read this chapter, you are ready for action. So, let's get it done.

With love, Ivana & Kristína

The detailed plan

If you have 6 months to complete a task, it will take you 6 months. However, if you give yourself 10 hours for the same task, you will finish it in 10 hours. This is possible because you will not waste time on non-essential details. This concept is known as Parkinson's law, which Cyril Northcote Parkinson initially published in *The Economist* in 1955.[30] More than a half-century later, it still works.

Every time you think you cannot do this in 10 hours, remember that this is just the beginning. You can spend weeks analysing competition or crafting your content plan or preparing a LinkedIn communication, or you can set up a timer for an hour and start there. You can spend weeks crafting your content plan or prepare a LinkedIn communication draft in 1 hour. It's your choice.

By using the 10-hour Launch Plan, you will get the push you need to start. Each activity serves a purpose and is supported by the other activities. This is no coincidence. We have worked on this process for more than a decade. You just need to follow the activities in a particular order. We have included only what is necessary to start, nothing more.

Hour 1: Personal and Project goals

Knowing and seeing the goals constantly is crucial for the success of this Project. Each Ambassador, including you, has their own goals, as does the whole company. In Chapters 1 and 2, you have defined all of them.

---

30 N Parkinson, 'Parkinson's Law' (originally published in *The Economist*, 19 November 1955), www.economist.com/news/1955/11/19/parkinsons-law, accessed 10 September 2023

Let's focus on your company goal first. To start your Ambassador Project, choose the one goal that is the most important. We use our Proprietary Goal Creating System. First, we look inside the company for these answers:

- What are your sales/business goals for next year?

- What are your HR goals for next year?

- Do you have your biggest business obstacle defined?

- What about your competitors? Are they active on LinkedIn?

After we have a picture of the whole company, we then look outside. We continuously analyse the competition both in the region and globally. If you are a pioneer, you do not want to copy your competition. Find your inspiration in other sectors and areas of business.

Do your research, find external data and create tangible goals that are motivating and interesting for your Project Guardian. This way, you will have more resources allocated to your Project. When you present the results after a year, you want to show your team's progress and the impact this Project has had on your company. Think in numbers. Show a big purpose and a huge impact. Even the most ambitious goals can become a reality with the Ambassador Project.

Hour 2: Organise and prepare the kick-off meeting

We admit that it's easier for a third party to sell this Project to your colleagues as an opportunity of a lifetime. But your goal here is to reframe the idea of 'painful social media activities' to 'a privilege and opportunities generating investment of time'. Talk about this Project across the company. You might be surprised who will be your perfect Ambassador or game-changing Cheerleader. Put everyone in one room (physically or virtually) and explain why this Project is happening right now. Give your colleagues numbers and statistics and present your company goals. Show them the basics of how to use LinkedIn.

The kick-off meeting can be part of a strategic company event or a regular breakfast teambuilding event with a specific topic. Here is a checklist of what your colleagues should know after your kick-off meeting.

- What is an Ambassador Project?
- Why is it happening in the company now?
- Who is responsible for the Project?
- What are the company goals?
- How can each colleague support the results?
- What is in it for the company, the team and all the colleagues?

- What is the role of the Ambassador, and who is it for?

- How can your colleagues apply, and what are the criteria for choosing the team?

At the end of the kick-off meeting, tell colleagues what to do next. If they do not want to become Ambassadors, they should be aware of how to support the activities of the Ambassador Team. For those who want to be Ambassadors, give them a clear call to action: 'Send me an email by this Friday if you want to be an Ambassador.' Tell them that you will choose the final list of Ambassadors and that it is a privilege to become one.

TOP TIP

Do not dive deep into 'click here' technical information or they will start to think about tactical issues and lose focus. You will address all tactical questions later in the Project. Remember, you want this session as a strategic presentation; each step leads to another and a clear call to action.

Hour 3: Ambassador Project roles and their goals

You already know who The Project Hero and The Project Guardian are. After reading Chapter 2, you know exactly who your perfect Ambassador would be. You may already have some colleagues in mind. After the kick-off meeting, see if they want to participate. Remember that you want Ambassadors who are committed. If you feel hesitation, trust your gut and let them be active Cheerleaders. You do not want any team member to leave in the next year because it wasn't their priority.

Finalise the four roles after the kick-off meeting. Now refer to Chapter 2 to see the best practices for choosing Ambassadors and how to help them define their goals.

Do not forget to track progress. Prepare an Ambassador Project Spreadsheet with all measured data on the day the Project starts, including future goals. We highly recommend adding monthly or quarterly milestones. This Project Spreadsheet should be accessible to the whole team at all times. This is how they can track their progress, and it can serve as a Leaderboard to ignite competitiveness.

Our client, multinational insurance company Generali, had every Ambassador fill out the Spreadsheet by themselves on the last day of each month. They added the links to their posts, the number of views after one week and other milestones and goals.

Hour 4: Structure for your LinkedIn presence (Company Pages and personal profiles)

Which unique structure is the best for your company? One Global LinkedIn Company Page, a variety of Company Pages, or a balanced combination of a few pages? Which personal profiles will be included in this Project? Do you want your board or leadership team to have a professional personal profile, even if these colleagues will not be Ambassadors?

Draft a simple structure. All you need is a pen and paper. Make it visual. Add the names of admins and their support team to each Company Page.

Now think about the visual umbrella for your unique structure. Take profile photos for your Ambassadors, Cheerleaders and Company Page. Organise a company photoshoot. You don't need fancy equipment and a large production team, but it is essential that the photos have the same vibe.

Hour 5: Put social media guidelines in place

An official Ambassador Project means more engagement, action and preparation. Check whether your company has social media guidelines for your Project team. We do not mean the sixty-page document sitting somewhere where no one knows about it. If you have a communications department or global marketing team with rules for social media, use them and modify it for this Project.

If you are starting with Employee Ambassadors, make sure to cover these topics, preferably in a one- to two-page document:

- Who can use social media at work

- Where to find resources – training and content hub

- The best practices for content creation (including copyright, intellectual property and legal consequences)

- Dos and don'ts

- Information that is prohibited from sharing (clients, non-public financial information, legal information, strategies, etc)

- What to do when something goes wrong

TOP TIP

If you do not have guidelines, start with a draft of straightforward ones you can create in 1 hour. Cover the points that are the most relevant to your company and situation. You will reiterate this as you progress with the Project.

Hour 6: Draft a LinkedIn communication strategy

Consistency, consistency, consistency. That is the golden rule of LinkedIn communication. It pleases the algorithm and keeps the Project alive. During this hour, write down five topics you want to cover on your Company Page(s) and three topics for each Ambassador. You will need this for your first meeting with the Ambassadors in Hour 7.

Prepare any critical information for your Ambassadors to share during your first meeting. We highly recommend setting up your Content Library. This makes approving pictures, videos and other content formats effortless. Make sure Ambassadors can access it any time.

From our experience, giving Ambassadors as much freedom as possible is always good. If they can be creative, their content will be written from the heart and reach much more than 'corporate content'. Your task is to set the tone of voice for LinkedIn communication. You can choose your company values as keywords your colleagues already know and live by. Ambassadors usually have experience in creating some content – maybe not for social media, but for a blog or a newspaper. Help them to build their authentic voice, but please do not force them to communicate as the company expects.

Trust your judgement about Ambassador selection and show them you trust them too. Teach them to tag the Company Page whenever they post something. This is how you can support them from your Company Page. You will also see where your company is mentioned and what the discussion is about.

Begin a list of contacts of colleagues they should talk to if they have questions or a particular problem. In most companies we have worked with, the primary contact is you – The Project Hero. If your Ambassador Project includes different countries, choose one responsible person in each country with one Global Project Superhero.

TOP TIP

Your team should know this rule of thumb: 'If it is safe to say something in an appointment with your competitor, then it is usually safe to use on LinkedIn.'

Hour 7: Prepare for the first Employee Ambassadors' meeting

Keep in mind that it is good to have the Project Guardian on your side to have your internal buy-in. Check all data, challenges and solutions before you go to the manager you think would be a perfect Project Guardian and ask them to attend your first Ambassadors' meeting.

The first Employee Ambassadors' meeting is the perfect place to present your LinkedIn communication strategy and next steps. Find 2 hours in your team's calendars and schedule it. You do not want to overwhelm your new team, but you need enough time to provide all the vital information.

Prepare notes for the meeting. Our best practice shows that these are the topics you want to include and tick off:

- Presentation of LinkedIn communication strategy

- Ambassadors' activities

- Presentation of their goals

- Schedule of the following meetings

- Education plan

- Primary knowledge transfer about profile, network and content

- What are the actions they need to take until your next meeting?

At the end of the session, your colleagues should know your expectations and how to meet them. Regular Ambassadors' meetings are the best way to get the most out of this Project. It's important to discuss achieving business goals and targets through LinkedIn, not just filling social media with information.

Hour 8: Prepare an education plan for the team

With knowledge comes power. Show your teammates that this Project matters by preparing an official education plan for the next 6 months. Topics we usually cover with our clients at the beginning of the Ambassador Project are:

- Personal profiles
- Connections, followers and networking best practices
- LinkedIn tech and data
- Generating content ideas
- How to support company content
- The LinkedIn algorithm and making your content more visible

You want to cover these topics in the first one to two months. Then you can move to more advanced ones like:

- Inbound vs outbound strategies
- Creating content that converts
- Getting colleagues to support your content
- Building meaningful relationships
- Engaging people to follow and connect with
- Advanced sales/HR/brand building strategies

After the initial training schedule, set dates at least once per quarter. This will help your team stay current, as there are new LinkedIn features and trends every few months. Do the schedule now because your Ambassadors will be busy, that is certain. Schedule non-negotiable meetings 3 to 6 months in advance.

When you have your education plan, your team members will see how important this Project is, and they will put more effort into it. Learning and progress are one of the best motivators.

Hour 9: Start the content creation

As the Project Hero, you need to lead by example. Creating the structure for your colleagues is not enough. Show your fellow Ambassadors that you also do what you tell them to do and be a true inspiration. If you have not visited your LinkedIn profile for a few years, you need to get started and take action yourself. Your action will get all others on board.

Content is important. We've got your back – that's why we created the 5-ingredient method for content creation. Everything you need to know, from the ultimate algorithm tip to AI, is in Chapters 4 and 5. Content creation can be, and should be, fun. Show your team that you have started to create yourself. Challenge yourself, set a timer for 15 minutes and get it done. Prepare a short piece of content for your personal profile.

Then start the content creation for your team. Begin with the first ingredient: time pressure. Choose how to apply it to your Project in Chapter 4. You can, and will, modify it after some time. At the beginning of the Project, choose just one and implement it.

For the following four ingredients, prepare some examples for your colleagues. You can talk about it a million times, but if you show them, they will get more clarity, support and motivation. Again, a quick presentation will make a difference. Go back to Chapter 4, and after completing the action step, you will have your Hour 9 successfully done.

Hour 10: Build in the accountability and keep motivation going

Having an accountability partner gives your team an average 65% chance of meeting their goals. This increases to about 95% when you have ongoing meetings to report your progress. According to the American Society for Training & Development – success is practically guaranteed.[31] From our experience, accountability enormously affects the Ambassador

---

31 B Wissman, 'An Accountability Partner Makes You Vastly More Likely to Succeed', *Entrepreneur* (20 March 2018), www.entrepreneur.com/leadership/an-accountability-partner-makes-you-vastly-more-likely-to/310062, accessed 15 June 2023

Project, so it is the key ingredient in our 10-hour Launch Plan.

When you recognise your Ambassadors and Cheerleaders and reward their actions, creative ideas and published content, you will add an extra layer of fun while keeping all eyes on the goals.

We are proud holders of the Experience Product Certification. Our Employee Advocacy Programmes use seven psychological triggers in every step of this 10-hour Launch Plan. It brings gamification to the next level. Sometimes it's visible and at other times so subtle that the team does not even notice, but it makes a big difference. Some of the ideas that we implemented for our clients are:

1. **Challenges and leaderboards:** They track Ambassadors' progress on their personal KPIs and celebrate milestones and achievements regularly.

2. **Ambassadors' spotlights and peer recognition:** Featuring them on the LinkedIn Company Page, websites, newsletters and social media posts.

3. **Personalised training and workshops:** Covering a specific topic when they reach a goal.

4. **Building a global community:** Virtual events to connect with colleagues in other countries.

5. **Gamified rewards:** For example, professional photoshoots, gift cards, extra vacation days, tickets to events, bonuses, vacations.

If you want to motivate the Cheerleaders, start with an internal campaign. Create a content creation corner or a special board they can use as a background. For example, some of our clients have motivational boards with hashtags, motivational quotes and praise to inspire their Cheerleaders. Show them how their activity helps the company and how it helps them personally. Highlight the company's social responsibility projects and how the Ambassador Project helps to spread the word.

When you connect employees' personal values to your company's mission, you create shared goals which are even more meaningful than individual metrics. If you support your company's Ambassadors' culture, the investment return is significant. You will increase employee satisfaction, decrease employee turnover, increase sales and much more.

✎ ACTION STEP

Take a moment to think of three specific strategies to motivate your Ambassadors and Cheerleaders.

Let's take a look at one of our clients that implemented the whole Ambassador Project. When you think about a bank and its internal and external communication, you usually visualise corporate, cold and professional but VÚB banka (Intesa Sanpaolo Group) is the perfect example of applying values like humanity or humour into the LinkedIn strategy.

CASE STUDY: VÚB BANKA (INTESA SANPAOLO GROUP)

The company had used LinkedIn as a tool for a long time but very rarely actively communicated on it. The bank's LinkedIn profile did not reflect a clearly defined brand and tone of voice used in communicating with clients. The Company Page was not used for employer branding or internal communication. The employees really loved working for VÚB banka (Intesa Sanpaolo Group), but they did not communicate this to the outside world. The LinkedIn Company Page was not used for employer branding at all. They decided to change that.

Why the Project started: The spark that started the amazing LinkedIn journey was the acute need for new colleagues, mainly from the IT sector. They had great teams and a working environment, but the company did not communicate this. The tone of voice for B2C marketing campaigns was very warm. Using humour, they attracted a specific type of client and wanted to attract a specific type of talent, too.

The implementation process: The company went through the whole Ambassador Project in the stages we defined in this book. They started with almost the entire HR department and other groups of employees. After they'd identified their perfect Ambassadors from various departments (the Board, PR, HR, IT and the contact centre), their Ambassadors had a unique content creation support programme, education plan and regular meetings. The Ambassadors also had the chance to impact the Company Page.

The Marketing and PR department created an internal campaign for colleagues that presented LinkedIn's importance with practical tips. LinkedIn was added to the recruitment and onboarding process to give candidates a chance to find out what it looks like inside the company and thus achieve a better fit with the company culture.

The biggest changes in their LinkedIn communication were:

- Authentic pictures without any major adjustments from an advertising agency
- Every Ambassador created posts for their personal profiles by themselves
- Internal support from Cheerleaders increased the impact of both internal and external communication

The results:

- Regionally, the company reached the highest engagement rate in the banking sector
- 400+% increase in the number of followers of the Ambassadors
- Significant increase of IT-experienced followers on the Company Page
- LinkedIn became an effective platform for internal communication and retention
- They receive a stream of incoming CVs that are an excellent fit for the company culture
- Receiving various awards for the company and their Ambassadors (including Best Employer Award)

THE MAGIC OF EMPLOYEE INFLUENCE

- Global impact by means of informal communication of important activities and projects to their parent company

---

Summary

In this chapter, we have covered the 10-hour Launch Plan. We focused on the following:

- The need for creating this plan

- A personal letter to you, our Hero

- How to prepare the 10-hour Launch Plan hour by hour

- Exact activities during these hours

- Showing you how many months' worth of work can be done within a week

Now you have the magic formula, and you are ready to fly!

But wait, are you ready for even more? Then the next chapter is for you.

SEVEN

Think Big, Think Global

You love to think big. We know this because you are reading Chapter 7. It means you want to take your colleagues' advocacy to the next level. What's exciting is that it does not matter if you are a company of two or twenty thousand. It is how big your vision is that counts.

This chapter is a bonus for those who like challenges and want to think big. Here, we will show you that there is more you can get from your LinkedIn presence and what to do about it.

The tone of voice and cultural differences

There are countries in which certain social media platforms are banned or inaccessible; others have very strict privacy policies. For example, in Europe, strict GDPR regulations will influence what private information, including name, pictures and videos, you can or cannot use in your content.

Certain topics are sensitive or taboo in some cultures, and it's important that you are aware of these. For example, in some countries it is common to use humour or sarcasm in business, but in others it is considered inappropriate. Topics that resonate in one region may not be relevant for others, or they may be offensive. Some cultures value modesty, and others prefer confidence. You need to know this when you create content. Therefore, it's crucial to have Local Project Heroes who will make sure that the content and messaging are tailored for a particular region. Reflect on the cultural values of a region and you will build more trust and credibility while reaching your goals.

How do you find new topics to start and follow in a new market? You:

- Join the discussion under interesting posts
- Search for LinkedIn events in that country and connect with participants and hosts

- Create more – the comments will become your new posts

- Become industry famous across borders

- Build your community in the new market by engaging with content

Start planning

When you implement the 10-hour Launch Plan and see the Project growing, you may feel tempted to take it global. We have been there – feeling the urge to help more people. Listen to your gut instinct and think about how you can help people on the other side of the world using the power of your colleagues' voices.

We have seen many clients do the same. Some of them knew they wanted to go global from the beginning. Others quietly pitched their idea to their board and were amazed when they got permission to scale up their Ambassador Project in various regions.

✎ ACTION STEP

Coordinating a Global Ambassador Project is not easy, but answering these questions will give you some guidance:

- How can you help people not only in your country, but globally?

- What will this Project look like if it goes better than you have ever imagined?
- What is the most significant result you can think of?

You need a great system and structure to take this Project globally, but if there is anyone who can do it, it's you. You know what it takes to plan and execute a local Ambassador Project, and with this experience and these skills, helping your colleagues worldwide will be extremely valuable.

Take what you have learned in your region and let your global colleagues follow the 10-hour Launch Plan. Be by their side and transfer your knowledge in a way that empowers them to be seen. Make it structured, easy to follow and fun. This chapter will show you how to modify the 10-hour Launch Plan for global impact. Consider it a completely new project, not just an add-on. Let's call it the Global Ambassador Project.

You can launch the Global Project in just 10 hours too. We began our discussion on how to scale the Ambassador Project globally in Chapter 5. Now let's dig into the details.

To give you accurate advice for the best Ambassador Project structure, we need to know your vision, current goals, ideal leads, sales/candidate funnels, guidelines and policies, team structure and more.

Our job as consultants is to understand the specifics of your company and current situation and give you the advice to get powerful results. In Chapter 5, we showed you that some structures for your LinkedIn presence are more advanced and complicated; some are simpler. There is no 'one size fits all', so for now, let's look at the easiest way to build your Global Ambassador team.

Common questions

Question 1: What languages should Ambassadors use for their personal profiles?

Personal profiles can be created in multiple languages, but for the Global Ambassador Project, we recommend that your Ambassadors use English along with the primary language used in their region. So, people with English profiles see the English version, and those with the profile in your local language will see the one in the local language. For example, a German potential client with a German LinkedIn profile will see your German version.

When you choose to use two language versions, updating both profiles is more time-consuming, but it works. The other option is to have a profile in English, but create content in the local language. In general, creating content in the local language drives more engagement.

We asked over a thousand people if they minded reading the content of local experts in English, provided they were fluent. Seventy-two per cent said it does not matter, but we see two to five times more engagement when our clients use the local language. That's because it is easier to consume. In one country, you can also have Ambassadors who create content in different languages according to their ideal Leads.

Language differences can be a problem if the teams from other countries really want to support content, but don't understand it. Even though there is a Translate button and the translations are surprisingly accurate, they may stop being supportive after a while. But we have great news for you: it does not matter. Support from your global team members is needed the most at the beginning of a Global Project. After a while, each Ambassador will build their own strong, local community.

Question 2: Should we use multiple Company Pages?

When you already have multiple Company Pages, first audit which ones you need to reach your goals globally. There might be various regional profiles for a particular product/service range, product, subsidiary, daughter company, etc.

In Chapter 5, you will find more information about the three structures for a LinkedIn presence that you can create. If you want to have it as easy as possible, strive for Structure # 3 over time. That way, you will not have to create content for the whole global company in one place, colleagues in regions will feel empowered, and they can take ownership of their local pages.

Question 3: Should you have a multilingual Company Page and target specific countries?

With Company Page, you can target specific countries with local languages. That is an excellent option for companies using Structure # 1 from Chapter 5: One Global LinkedIn Company Page.

If that is you, let the regions provide you with relevant content. Do not try to push global content to regions that do not resonate. Cultural differences significantly impact how people communicate and engage with content.

Follow your social media guidelines, but you can give the regions more autonomy in posting. Make sure they know how often you expect them to come up with new content and what global goals they should support. ·

Question 4: Should you have local pages in the local language?

Sometimes the number one choice for companies is to have local pages in English. It depends on who your followers are. They may be local clients or global part-ners. Who do you want the most engagement from? Locals or English speakers? If it is local clients, then use the local language. If you are in a bilingual region, then English is your choice.

The local language is a better option for engagement and results in general. It does not mean you must choose your Company Page language and keep it like that forever. Test which type of content and language your followers, and particularly your ideal Leads, prefer. Over the next two weeks, post in the local language for the first week and then in your local lan-guage the following week. It may take time to decide and that's fine. Just start and see where your followers lead you with their engagement.

Question 5: Do you start in one country or build Global Ambassadors simultaneously?

In Chapter 5, you learned that you have two main options when creating a Global Project:

- Create an Ambassador Team in one country and replicate in the future to other territories (this is the easier option).

- Create a full Global Ambassador Team with one Ambassador per country and then replicate it within other departments and territories. This is a more advanced version which needs more buy-in and coordination.

When you want to scale this Project, you can either replicate your Ambassador Team from your territory to others, or empower the one Ambassador in each country to replicate within other departments and regions.

Global Ambassador Project roles

When you take the Project globally, you need even more structure, accountability and collaboration, ensuring that everyone knows their responsibilities. This targeted approach supercharges productivity and ensures that every aspect of the Project receives the attention it deserves. The result? A comprehensive and impactful Employee Ambassadors' strategy that drives exceptional results. To do this, we need to introduce two new roles: the Global Project Guardian and the Global Superhero.

Global Project Guardian

The Global Project Guardian is a critical ally in driving the Project success and ensures buy-in across countries and managerial levels. The Project Guardian has substantial influence as a prominent figure within your leadership team, preferably at a global level. Look no further than key positions such as the CEO or other board members, the Head of Marketing or HR, or the Head of Digital. These individuals have the authority and strategic vision to champion your

Project, securing the necessary support and resources for its success on a global scale.

Global Superhero

Stepping into the role of a Global Superhero is like taking the helm of a ship sailing into new waters. You'll be managing the launch of this Project across multiple countries. It's a unique opportunity to extend your impact on a global scale.

It's important not to get too caught up in the tiny details. Your role is to keep an eye on the big picture, overseeing the whole project from a broader perspective. You're also a role model, representing the company's values and brand, and it's your job to get others excited about joining the Ambassadors' movement. Your role is to inspire your team, foster engagement and build a stronger, more connected global company community.

Local Project Hero

Why do you need your Local Project Hero? Local Project Heroes are an essential part of your team. They have a unique understanding of their people and the inner workings of the local company landscape. Despite the best efforts of a Global Superhero, grasping the intricate dynamics of teams, company insights and client relationships in each country can be challenging.

You need an insider – a Local Project Hero – who can efficiently steer the Project, provide critical information and handle enquiries from local colleagues. It isn't practical for you to field calls from team members in France, for instance, about how to adjust their privacy settings on LinkedIn. Instead, the Local Project Hero can take on these tasks, ensuring smoother operations.

The Ambassador

Content is the lifeblood of the Ambassador Project. Ambassadors are your key players when it comes to creating compelling content that captivates the target audience. They have an insider's perspective on your company, products and culture and help you to bridge the gap with potential clients and colleagues – let their enthusiasm be part of sharing your story.

The process of choosing Ambassadors for a Global Project is slightly different because of the cultural differences. Leave it to the Local Project Heroes but give them guidance how to do it right. Your invaluable experience from your Local Project will help them tremendously.

The Cheerleader

Your Cheerleaders amplify your Ambassadors' efforts and drive engagement with the target audience. They form a passionate army of supporters, some even taking the initiative to create their own compelling content. Their primary mission is to uplift others and, in time, potentially evolve into Ambassadors themselves. By providing them with the proper guidance and support, they have the power to nurture relationships, attract valuable clients and talent, and elevate your company's reputation through authentic and meaningful interactions.

If you have a few employees, it is easier to track the activity of your Cheerleaders. But what do you do when you have thousands, or even more, active LinkedIn users in your company? There is no way you can track this manually, but you can use smart Employee Ambassadors' software solutions. Reach out to us for insight on the most effective tools currently available and we'll get you set up with success.

Look at this visual example of a Global Project hierarchy to understand the structure and the different connections.

Now that we've defined what roles will be participating in this Project, here is our simple 5-step process to set up the Global Ambassador Project. This process is for the Global Superhero who will launch the Project. So, get your notebook ready and start planning.

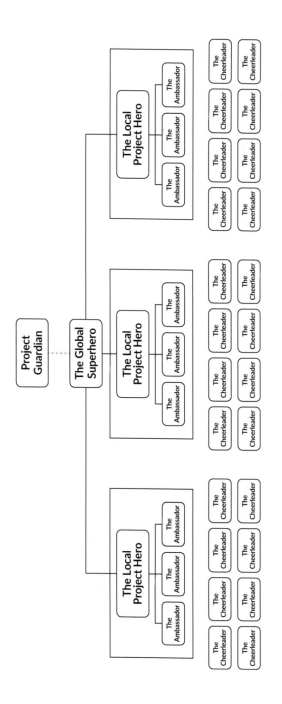

5-step process for the Global Superhero

Step 1: Global buy-in

You will probably have to prepare a business case for your leadership team to get global buy-in. What potential do you see for your company? What do you want to happen, and more importantly, why?

When you want to start a formal Global Ambassador Project, you will have colleagues who think the solution is to purchase cool software for sharing corporate content, and that's it. This may work for some companies, but the results of what your colleagues can make with their own stories and opinions are far superior. That's why preparing a business case to get leadership buy-in is vital.

Step 2: Find a Global Project Guardian

For a Global Ambassador Project to succeed, you need two fundamental components in Step 2: an influential supporter and a sizable budget. The first is a strong personality, someone who is not just an avid fan of your work but an advocate who can help drive your goals forward. This could be a high-profile leader who will help you attract massive managerial support.

The second crucial element is a substantial budget. Adequate funding allows you to create a significant and impactful Project. Again, your Project Guardian will help you access the necessary resources.

In essence, these two elements – an influential advocate and a solid budget – form the foundation of your Ambassador Project, setting you on the path to creating something truly impressive.

Step 3: Set goals

Imagine a year from now. How will you measure the success of this Project? What has to happen for this to be a global success? Go back to Chapter 1 and implement what you have learned about goal setting and measuring the success of this Project. The goals may be slightly or entirely different for different regions. For example, one may focus on recruiting top talent and the other on retention and reputation management. Cooperate with the Global Project Guardian and Local Project Heroes to ensure there are appropriate goals in place. Local goals will be defined in the 10-hour Launch Plan later in this chapter.

Step 4: Identify the regions and motivate to participate

Picture a team of highly engaged and motivated colleagues from around the world. If you empower your colleagues across different cultures, it will have stronger internal benefits. Your colleagues will share their knowledge and expertise, boosting their engagement, retention and confidence.

Think about the energy when you have a great team. What happens when someone with a negative attitude joins it? The energy, team motivation and productivity vanish. Therefore, finding individuals that fit the Global Project is quite a task. It all starts with ensuring the right countries are motivated to participate because they have big challenges they want to solve.

Step 5: Identify potential risks of your global strategy

The most common challenge is that the Project is so complex that your colleagues will lose ownership. Shared responsibility needs support from the Global Superhero, Local Project Heroes and, occasionally, empowerment from the Project Guardian. Define KPIs for each country, and it will keep your team on track. Start with the simplest KPIs, for example, the number of connections, followers, number of posts, etc. Then follow the tips in Chapter 1: 'Setting the Project goals and measuring results'.

10-hour Launch Plan modified for a global impact

Cultural differences, language barriers and diverse legal regulations may seem to make it challenging to create a unified strategy that can be applied globally, but we will give you a simple 10-hour Global Launch Plan to follow to help deal with these issues.

Show your Local Project Heroes how to follow it and empower colleagues globally with a system they can replicate after you launch the pilot.

Every region has its nuances, and this is where a Local Project Hero comes into play. Your job is to find a partner in each country, or at least every region, and help them to start with their own 10-hour Launch Plan.

Hour 1

Ask your Local Project Heroes to write their top five goals. Refer them to Chapter 1: 'Setting the Project goals and measuring results'. This is a new area, different to your home country, and new markets need new and local goals. Ask your Local Project Heroes to research local competition so that you will have a benchmark to start with. Then jump higher. Remember, the sky's the limit.

Hour 2

Prepare a kick-off meeting for Local Project Heroes. By now, you have already done the kick-off for all your colleagues. They know what LinkedIn is about and how to support your team's efforts. For this kick-off, do not bring other colleagues into the room, just the Local Project Heroes.

Hour 3

Choosing the right Ambassadors will be slightly different this time. Employee Ambassadors for global expansion should be pre-selected from your leadership team depending on their sales or HR strategy. Again, the best Ambassadors are those who want this role, not those who must be visible. And just a reminder, one Ambassador should not be responsible for managing multiple personal profiles of other Ambassadors.

Hour 4

Draft a simple structure of your Company Page and the personal profiles you will use. It is easiest to start with personal profiles. That is the beauty of the Ambassador Project. Until you make a decision about the whole structure, including various Company Pages, you can be more flexible with using personal profiles as a start.

Hour 5

An international faux pas is the last thing you need. Do not gamble with your company's reputation. You may already have your global social media guidelines in place. However, they need to be localised. During this hour, find people who will be responsible for localising them to particular regions.

Hour 6

Set up a meeting of Local Project Heroes and ask them to prepare their own local LinkedIn communication draft. It can be very similar to what you already have or it might be very different. The topics will be adapted to each country's sales or HR strategy, and you might be surprised by how different cultures see it. Let them take ownership of their strategy but give them the guidance they need.

Hour 7

The first Employee Ambassadors' meeting will be super exciting and a bit scary. You are making giant leaps and want to coordinate a much larger Project than before. Go to Chapters 1 and 2 and prepare data, prepare your arguments to prove it works and a checklist to make the first meeting successful.

Hour 8

In this Project, your Global Education Plan should start with a series of workshops. Start with basic ones and use advanced information over time. Follow the steps in Chapter 6. Behind an international project, there are always nuances. All Ambassadors should be aware of differences and shortcuts they can use.

Hour 9

Now here's the fun bit. During this hour, ask your Local Project Heroes to follow the 5-ingredient Method for content creation and schedule a coworking session to support them during content creation. Content repurposing can reach the next level if you are in a multilingual environment, so play with it more during your content coworking session.

Hour 10

Have you heard about the difference between motivation and stimulation? Motivation is long-term. It is something deep inside that helps us to get through a difficult period. It can be, for example, teamwork, education, colleague compliments or work enrichment. Stimulation is like fuel that speeds up progress. The easiest way to stimulate is by money, profit shares, etc. Look at the tips in Chapter 6 to keep your motivation going. During this hour, write down the top three ideas for motivating your Local Project Heroes and ask them to come up with three tips for encouraging their local Ambassadors.

Make a difference with a global impact

If you are reading this, it means you are ready. LinkedIn does not recognise borders. Building a Global Ambassador Project is like building a bridge connecting your company to a global clientele and

workforce simultaneously. It strengthens relationships internally and externally on a global level. If you
create a formal structure and support, your Ambassadors and Cheerleaders from all countries can support
each other. This will increase the Project's success rate
in a way that nothing else can.

And yes, you absolutely can make a difference even if
you're from a small country! We have seen it so many
times with our clients. Here are just two examples:

Picture one of the leading manufacturers globally creating space for dozens of their HR executives from
various countries. They discussed their local goals,
challenges and needs so that a common global
LinkedIn strategy could be formed. All from a city of
just 40,000 inhabitants.

Or our client, dm drogerie markt, that successfully
embarked on a cross-departmental and cross-country
LinkedIn employer branding transformation. They
changed the way they use LinkedIn in Europe and all
while in a small country like Slovakia.

Let´s look deeper into this success story.

CASE STUDY: DM DROGERIE MARKT

The company is Europe's premier drugstore retail
chain, renowned for its B2C retail stores and high-
quality products. In addition, the company is an
innovative employer, pioneering CSR initiatives, internal

educational projects, untraditional employee benefits and dual training for secondary school students.

The situation: B2C themes were being communicated on Instagram, Facebook and YouTube. Despite being a brand people love in retail and logistics, dm drogerie markt was largely unrecognised for its exciting opportunities in white-collar roles, particularly in the IT, Legal, Marketing and Expansion departments. The company's proud workforce needed a social platform to amplify their experiences, and potential high-quality recruits were largely unaware of the diverse career opportunities available.

The objective: The goal was to use LinkedIn to position dm drogerie markt as a top-tier employer for a wide range of professional talent. Key to this was a desire to showcase the company's sustainable practices, including zero-waste initiatives, to attract high-quality recruits aligned with the company's values.

The starting point: Before the inception of the Ambassador Project, LinkedIn was utilised mainly on an individual basis, with a passive Company Page created to be followed by existing employees. Recognising the platform's potential, the top management gave the green light for a dedicated LinkedIn strategy led by two colleagues from the HR department, with leaders from various departments committing to active participation.

The strategy: A cross-departmental Ambassador Project Group was formed, with key representatives from the C-suite (CIO, CFO, CHRO, CMO) and HR department. The team set out to:

- Highlight the distinctive work culture at dm drogerie markt

- Start an Ambassadors and communication initiative on LinkedIn
- Engage top management as active Ambassadors.
- Elevate Ambassador profiles for greater visibility and connectivity
- Regularly create engaging content for both the Company Page and personal profiles
- Regularly connect with colleagues from other European countries to build a cross-cultural project that aligned with the strategy, vision and values of the company

The execution: The Ambassador Team launched a comprehensive campaign that integrated personal storytelling, values-led content and active networking. This cross-departmental effort fostered a shared sense of purpose within the organisation and created an inclusive atmosphere where everyone felt equally important.

The impact: The results of the Ambassador Project were not only transformative but also far-reaching and resulted in:

- The doubling of followers on the Company Page
- A surge in monthly engagement, increasing by up to 500%
- A 300% organic increase in connections on Ambassadors' personal profiles
- Six-figure view counts on LinkedIn Company Page posts
- Creative posts that drew in high-quality candidates

The global impact: After a year, the Employee Ambassadors had the necessary tools, strategies, and tactics to continue the initiative. The success of this small subsidiary in transforming employer branding through LinkedIn inspired larger European entities within the group to adopt similar strategies. This cross-country project led to forming an 'Attractive Employer Working Group' across various European countries, including Austria, the Czech Republic, Germany and Italy. This formalised project approach further amplified the company's attractiveness as an employer on an international scale.

The HR department started receiving proactive requests from employees seeking more LinkedIn training and reinforcing internal communication with social proof. Significant increases in visitors to both the website and career page from LinkedIn demonstrated the campaign's success. But beyond the numbers, the initiative fostered a more connected, empowered workforce at dm drogerie markt, highlighting the far-reaching impact of a successful cross-departmental, cross-country project.

Summary

This chapter is for those who think big. We have covered:

- How to start planning a Global Ambassador Project

- Answers to the most common questions when it comes to a Global Ambassador Project

- Extra roles needed for a Global Project

- A 5-step process for Global Superheroes

- Modification of the 10-hour Launch Plan

Conclusion

Be honest. Did you believe you could prepare and launch an Ambassador Project in such a short time when you started to read this book? We promise that your results will leave you speechless when you implement the 10-hour Launch Plan.

So just keep going. For every obstacle, you will find a solution in this book. Get creative, have fun and follow the proven process.

You have found the unique ingredients and ways to unite the team, set up the system, and keep them going. And what is most important: to bring joy to this Project. Knowing 'how' leaves you more time for each team member and their particular needs. Make sure they not only feel valued but supported and heard.

You've learned that there are four roles in the Project and the unique path of every member of your Ambassador Team. You know how to choose the right Ambassadors and define their personal and company goals.

In the 10-hour Launch Plan, we prepared the exact steps to guide you through the Project. Follow them, and you cannot get lost. Show your team members why this Project is critical and, especially, what they can get from it. Help them to define their goals and motivate them to reach them.

Provide all the knowledge they need to represent your company in the right tone of voice. Show them how they should communicate and be their support during the Project. Help them be more visible because content creation in this Project is the key. This is the most complex task for your Ambassadors. To be consistent, they need more than just a few pieces of information at the beginning. Get creative and keep their motivation going. If now is the right time, make your Project international, or even global.

We've got your back if you need help with your Ambassador projects. Let's talk if you get stuck. We can help you through the following:

- Strategic sessions for the leadership teams
- Implementation of all steps in your launch plan

- 30-day social selling programmes

- 30-day employer branding programmes

- VIP days for C-level executives

- Tools, guidelines and toolkits for your Ambassadors and Cheerleaders

- Content creation sessions for your Ambassador teams

- Tailor-made LinkedIn retreats and experiences

Now you have everything you need to create a successful Ambassador Project in your company. Go through the action steps you wrote in your notebook and reread this book whenever necessary. Every minute you invest in your Employee Ambassadors will return multiple times. It is not easy, but you are brave enough to start a spark in your company. And you are skilled enough to become the most influential Ambassador in your field on LinkedIn.

Now go and make the magic happen.

Resources

Check out:

- ✓ our current programmes that can support you in this Ambassador adventure:
www.sundayflies.com

- ✓ a playlist of our selected interviews, podcasts and LinkedIn mood music:
https://bit.ly/sundayflies_spotify

- ✓ free additional resources to implement what you have read:
www.themagicofemployeeinfluence.com

Acknowledgements

Dear reader, thank you for deciding to amplify your and your colleagues' powerful voice. It takes courage, but we know you are brave and you can do it.

Lucy and Joe, thank you for creating an amazing streamlined process where we became authors without being stuck for years. Siobhan, you made months of writing this book joyful and fun and supported us when it got tough. We were looking forward to each one of our feedback sessions that were invaluable. Vicky, Anke and the whole team, thank you for polishing our final version.

Thank you, dear clients, for your courage to be trendsetters with your Employee Ambassadors, your trust to be a part of your LinkedIn journey and allowing us to share your experience in this book. Thanks to you, LinkedIn is a place full of inspiration, opportunities and fun.

Thank you, dear beta readers, for devoting your time to help us make this book an ultimate guideline our readers can rely on.

Special thanks go to our loved ones who supported us. Mum and Dad, thank you for everything you have done for us; you gave us life, showed us what matters, and we will be forever grateful to have you in our lives. To our dear husbands, for supporting every crazy idea and especially for the place in your hearts we call home. To our four boys who made the writing of this book an amazing adventure. You all make our endeavours worth it.

The Authors

Meet Ivana

 Ivana was a top-tier head-hunter before she became a recognised expert on gamified employee advocacy with both a Masters and a PhD in Marketing and Business. She loves business and successfully began her entrepreneurial journey before she even started elementary school.

She founded her own head-hunting company at the young age of twenty-two. For a decade, she has interviewed thousands of people and learned to ask the right questions to dig deep into what drives people, what brings them joy at work and how to choose the right person for any project based on questions others have found strange (like whether they prefer to cook or to bake, and why!).

Ivana excelled in finding candidates for difficult-to-fill positions, so her clients started to ask how it was possible that she could fill vacancies they were not able to fill for many months. And so, in 2013, the first consultancy for building brands on LinkedIn was born.

Ivana has the ability to easily get people on board with ideas and projects, see the potential in others and naturally lead them to the next level of accomplishment. She keeps her eye on the company goals and personal objectives of the team, so that they will not get distracted and achieve what they want in the shortest amount of time possible.

She often travels, because it brings her joy and fresh perspectives, and dances as though her life depends on it – because it does. She loves to play. And she plays to win.

Meet Kristína

Kristína is a multi-talented and creative renowned expert on gamified employee advocacy passionate about engaging teamwork and streamlining processes, with a Masters in International Trade and a PhD in Management. She has diverse experience across various industries, from small companies to multinational corporations, including a Big4 consultancy, one of the best advertising agencies in the region and a premium car importer for Mercedes.

Kristína has played a vital role in working with leadership teams and stakeholders to design and implement effective procedures and processes to maximise businesses' time and resources. She loves simplifying complex ideas and elevating the tiny and quirky details that (not so surprisingly) ultimately become the business driving force for her clients.

The highest value she delivers during a project is inspiring people to become involved advocates. Her cheerful nature, vivid stories and passion keep everyone emotionally connected and empowered in the result. She makes sure that everyone, even the quietest coworker, is heard.

She will make sure your Ambassador Project is rooted in systems, tools and processes so that you and your colleagues can fully express your creativity without waiting for the muse to strike.

Beyond her professional accomplishments, Kristína is a multitalented creative who loves to paint. With her diverse skillset and passion for elevating people, Kristína is the perfect partner to show you the power of Employee Ambassadors on the scale.

Sisters Powerhouse

We were raised in an entrepreneurial family and were taught to honour gentlemen's agreements, to be true pioneers and to value simple family life. We may be sisters, but we are very different, like day and night, with unique experiences, different worldviews and approaches to new technology. We share the same values – family, courage, integrity, growth, adventure and simplicity. We both love to learn and grow.

After we joined forces in 2015, we created the first consultancy for building brands on LinkedIn in Slovakia, and in 2022 rebranded it to SUNDAYFLIES. For over a decade, we have empowered our clients to use their voice to attract opportunities and talent systematically and in record time, while still having fun. We are keynote speakers at top business conferences and regularly give interviews in podcasts and media, including *Forbes*. We are proud advocates of gami-fied principles and holders of the Experience Product Certifications. That means we have integrated ten core experiences to effectively stimulate action and engagement. By harnessing these strategies, we can create a dynamic and immersive environment that drives results and captures the attention.

We have hosted the largest LinkedIn event in our region for several years. Now we focus on creating global brand architecture on LinkedIn and LinkedIn training for companies like Lidl, dm drogerie markt, EY, Henkel, ING Hubs, Generali, SAS, CloudTalk and many others.

🌐 www.sundayflies.com

🔗 www.linkedin.com/company/sundayflies

🔗 www.linkedin.com/in/ivanabrutenic/

🔗 www.linkedin.com/in/kristinacichykovacikova/